New England

A Guide To The State & National Parks

Barbara Sinotte

HUNTER
PUBLISHING

Hunter Publishing, Inc.
300 Raritan Center Parkway
Edison NJ 08818, USA
Tel (908) 225 1900
Fax (908) 417 0482

ISBN 1-55650-738-0

© 1996 Hunter Publishing

Maps by Kim André

Cover photo by Henryk T. Kaiser

Other titles in the Parks' Series include:
ARIZONA & NEW MEXICO, CALIFORNIA, COLORADO,
NEW YORK & NEW JERSEY, OREGON & WASHINGTON

Contents

A Word About Hiking...

CONNECTICUT

A Word About Hiking...

Hiking is by far the most popular activity in state and national parks. Most of the trails are clearly marked. Off-trail travel (commonly referred to as bushwhacking) is practiced by the more adventurous hikers – especially in the less-populated areas.

Trails in many state parks have been rated by taking into consideration the length of the hike and the degree of difficulty. If you are not sure which trails are appropriate for you and your family, talk to a park ranger. If you do not exercise regularly, start on beginner trails and increase your distances gradually. Trail maps are usually available either at the trail head or at the ranger station.

While trail signs vary widely, there are a few common markings that everyone should be familiar with. Periodic paint blazes on trees or rocks are clearly the most popular indication of a trail. Plastic markers are often nailed to trees or metal signs or attached to their own wooden posts. Where there are no trees, trails are often marked with piles of rocks.

Watch for trail markers and make a habit of looking for them – for your own safety and the safety of those hiking with you. It does not take away from the enjoyment of hiking and will soon become just another "natural" thing to do.

If you want to go bushwhacking, be careful. Make your first attempts in open areas with limited undergrowth – such as a desert area where the terrain is a little easier to tackle. Bushwhacking through areas of dense vegetation is for the more experienced hiker and should only be attempted with map, water, and compass in hand.

Whether you are bushwhacking or following marked trails, set a comfortable pace for yourself. You are not in a race and can better take in the surroundings if you don't rush your excursion. Attempting to go too fast can ruin all the fun and burn you out before you are half-way through your hike. Stumbling or tripping is a clear sign that you may indeed need to slow down.

Remember to take frequent rest stops. Don't wait for fatigue to tell you it's time to slow down. A 10- to 15-minute stop every hour or so is a good idea when you begin. After a while, you will know what is best for you.

Don't speed over the rough areas of a trail. Watch out for tree roots and old logs that may be damp and slippery. If you are not sure of your footing, it is wise to crouch just a bit, lowering your center of gravity to reduce the likelihood of falling. Steep trails have caused many hikers to loose their balance and take a tumble. Descending tends to be more hazardous than ascending and requires a little more attention. Hold onto small trees or rocks. When in doubt, sitting and easing your way down on your rear might be the way to go.

It is important to choose a trail that is comfortable for everyone. Younger children should be introduced to hiking with short walks. It is more fun and educational if they can be involved in planning the hike.

Checklist for a Day of Hiking

Hiking boots
Day pack
Water bottle
Waterproof poncho
Extra sweater
Snack foods
Toilet paper
Plastic litter bag
2 pairs of hiking socks
Liner socks
Long pants
Long-sleeved shirt
Shell parka or windbreaker

In summer you should include:
T-shirt
Shorts
Extra water
Bug repellant
Sunscreen or lotion
Sun hat

In cool or cold weather add:
Additional layers
Cap or hat
Thermal underwear

When hiking without a group of friends add:
Map
Trail guidebook
Compass
First aid kit
Flashligh
Pocket knife
Matches
Watch

Hiking Safety

- Hike with a friend.
- Take plenty of drinking water.
- Let someone at the camp or at home know where you are going and when you plan to return.
- Don't take shortcuts on a switchback trail.

Connecticut

State Parks

Connecticut measures 90 miles east to west, 75 miles north to south, with the Connecticut River cutting the state in half. It is rolling and hilly and ever changing. It is tiny, to say the least, but this wonderful state offers some of the best kept parks and forests anywhere and will not disappoint you. Some of the parks are only as big as your back yard, but they offer sanctuary for birds and wildlife – and even city-weary urban dwellers.

State Agencies

The Department of Environmental Protection maintains all of the state's natural resources. For further information contact them at: 165 Capitol Ave., Hartford, CT 06106.

The Office of State Parks and Recreation is responsible for recreation areas in State Parks and State Forests. You can reach them at ☎ (203) 566-2304.

Algonquin State Forest

Location: From Winsted, head north on SR 8 for 1½ miles and follow the signs.

You may wonder why anyone would visit this state forest. It is closed to hunting and has few, if any, respectable fishing streams.

There are no trails to speak of. Bushwhacking is the only way to go. But the birds! It's described in Billard's *Places to Look for Birds* as a good place to see warblers in spring and fall. It is a sight to behold, and birdwatchers will have trouble finding a more perfect, unspoiled location.

For further information contact: Office of State Parks and Recreation, 165 Capitol Ave., Hartford, CT 06106. ☎ (203) 566-2304.

Bluff Point Coastal Reserve

Location: From I-95, Exit 88 to Route 117 S.

The Reserve is a bluff overlooking Mumford Cove, Long Island Sound, and the Poquonock River. The wooded highland descends to tidal wetlands. A long, narrow sandspit curves westward, ending at Bushy Point, a small island.

For further information contact: Office of State Parks and Recreation, 165 Capitol Ave., Hartford, CT 06106. ☎ (203) 566-2304.

Campbell Falls State Park

Location: On the Connecticut/Massachusetts border off Route 272 N.

A short trail through a delightful hemlock forest leads right into Massachusetts at Campbell State Park. The 50-ft. falls on Ginger Creek drop into a narrow ravine.

For further information contact: Office of State Parks and Recreation, 165 Capitol Ave., Hartford, CT 06106. ☎ (203) 566-2304.

Chatfield Hollow State Park

Location: From I-95 at Clinton, exit 63 N or SR 81 to Killingsworth.

This small park adjoins part of the Cockaponset State Forest and offers 18 miles of hiking trails, including the blue-blazed Chatfield Trail. A seven-acre pond provides fishing and swimming.

For further information contact: Office of State Parks and Recreation, 165 Capitol Ave., Hartford, CT 06106. ☎ (203) 566-2304.

Cockaponset State Forest

Location: From Chester, 3 miles west on SR 148.

The state's second largest State Forest extends for about 10 miles north to south on both sides of SR 9 in the western Connecticut River Valley.

Camping: 25 sites.
Hiking: The blue-blazed Cockaponset Trail runs north to south in the Turkey Hill block.
Hunting: Grouse, cottontail, deer, squirrel, raccoon, and waterfowl.
Fishing: Trout fishing.
Ski touring: Trails and unplowed roads.

For further information contact: Office of State Parks and Recreation, 165 Capitol Ave., Hartford, CT 06106. ☎ (203) 566-2304.

Connecticut River

Location: Stretching 70 river miles from the Massachusetts border to Long Island Sound.

Over 400 miles in length, the Connecticut River is New England's longest and most popular. Due to efforts to reduce pollution anadromous fish (those that migrate from salt water to spawn in fresh water) have re-appeared in the lower river. Hopes are always high that conditions will improve. The state provides opportunities for canoe camping along the lower river.

Camping: Reservations must be made at least two weeks in advance. One night only. No vehicle access.
Canoeing: Outfitting and transportationprovided at Gillette.
Boating: State launch sites at Enfield, Haddam Meadows, Old Saybrook Salmon River, Suffield, and Windsor.

For further information contact: Office of State Parks and Recreation, 165 Capitol Ave., Hartford, CT 06106. ☎ (203) 566-2304.

Devil's Hopyard State Park

Location: North of the junction of Routes 82 and 156 SE of Millington.

The chief attraction here is Chapman Falls, where Eight Mile River plunges down a 60-ft. escarpment.

Camping: 20 sites.
Hiking: Approximately 15 miles of trails lace the park.
Fishing: Brook trout.

For further information contact: Office of State Parks and Recreation, 165 Capitol Ave., Hartford, CT 06106. ☎ (203) 566-2304.

Durham Meadows Wildlife Management Area

Location: Near Wallingford. From I-91 exit 15 east on SR 68 to Durham then south on SR 17 to entrance.

Most of Durham Meadows is marsh along the Coginchaug River, partly overgrown in swamp maple.

Hunting: Pheasant, woodcock, waterfowl, squirrel.
Canoeing: Best in spring. Put-in is on SR 147, west of N block entrance.

For further information contact: Western District, Wildlife Bureau, 230 Plymouth Rd., Harwinton, CT 06791. ☎ (203) 485-0226.

Edward Steichen Memorial Wildlife Preserve

Location: From Route 15, exit 40 onto Route 7 N. The park is near Topstone.

The Preserve includes a red maple swamp, shrubby swamp, and uplands. A boardwalk enters the swamp.

For further information contact: Connecticut Audubon Society, 2325 Burr St., Fairfield, CT 06430. ☎ (203) 259-6305.

Gay City State Park

Location: From US 384, exit 5 then 3 miles south of Bolton.

This rolling, forested park has 10 numbered trails, offering a variety of hikes. The routes connect with the Shenipsit Trail, which runs from Cobalt through the Meshomasic and Shenipsit State Forests (see below) to the Massachusetts border.

For further information contact: Office of State Parks and Recreation, 165 Capitol Ave., Hartford, CT 06106. ☎ (203) 566-2304.

Hammonasset Beach State Park

Location: From 1-95, Exit 62.

This state park has two miles of Long Island Sound beach and the state's largest campground. In the spring and fall Meigs Point has shore and marsh birds. The extensive marsh on the Hammonasset attracts waterfowl, herons, and clapper rail.

Camping: 558 sites.
Fishing: Saltwater species.

For further information contact: Office of State Parks and Recreation, 165 Capitol Ave., Hartford, CT 06106. ☎ (203) 566-2304.

Henipsit State Forest

Location: From Stafford Springs, west about 6 miles on SR 190.

The Trail crosses the Forest's highest point: 1,121-ft. Bald Mountain and 1,061-ft. Soapstone Mountain. Terrain is moderately steep slopes, rock outcrops, ledges, small streams, and ponds.

Hunting: Grouse, woodcock, cottontail, squirrel, deer.
Ski touring: Trails and unplowed roads (very popular).

For further information contact: Office of State Parks and Recreation, 165 Capitol Ave., Hartford, CT 06106. ☎ (203) 566-2304.

Hopeville Pond State Park

Location: Exit 86 on the Connecticut Turnpike.

Camping: 81 sites.

For further information contact: Office of State Parks and Recreation, 165 Capitol Ave., Hartford, CT 06106. ☎ (203) 566-2304.

Housatonic State Forest/Housatonic Meadows State Park

Location: Several tracts on both sides of the Housatonic River on Route 7.

This State Park is along the west shore of the river. Campsites are set under pines on the river bank. Forest land adjoins the west boundary of the park. Another section across the river rises more than 700 ft. to the N-S ridge of Mine Mountain. From the Park, Pine Knob Loop, 2½ miles, climbs to a viewpoint at 1,160 ft.

Camping: 102 sites in the State Park.
Hiking/Backpacking: Parts of Appalachian Trail and local trails.
Hunting/Fishing: Grouse, pheasant, woodcock, cottontail, gray squirrel, raccoon, deer, and wild turkey. Trout in the River.

For further information contact: Office of State Parks and Recreation, 165 Capitol Ave., Hartford, CT 06106. ☎ (203) 566-2304.

Hurd State Park

Location: On east side of the Connecticut River near Middleton off Route 66.

This is a park with a picnic shelter and 2½ miles of woodland trails in two loops: one river-side, one to the Split Rock viewpoint.

Camping: Boat access only. Primitive sites.

For further information contact: Office of State Parks and Recreation, 165 Capitol Ave., Hartford, CT 06106. ☎ (203) 566-2304.

James L. Goodwin State Forest & Conservation Center

Location: On US 6, 3 miles east of South Chaplin.

Hiking: Easy hiking trails and roads in the woods. The Natchaug Trail crosses the Forest.
Fishing: Bass, bluegill, and bullheads.
Boating: Canoeing on flooded swamps.

For further information contact: Office of State Parks and Recreation, 165 Capitol Ave., Hartford, CT 06106. ☎ (203) 566-2304.

John A. Minnetto State Park

Location: Off SR 272 north of Torrington.

A central portion serves as a municipal park with such activities as picnicking, swimming, field sports, and winter sports. The other 500 acres are mostly wetland, with trails and good waterfowl viewing spots.

For further information contact: Office of State Parks and Recreation, 165 Capitol Ave., Hartford, CT 06106. ☎ (203) 566-2304.

Kettletown State Park/Indian Well State Park

Location: Exit 15 from Route 84. 5 miles south of Southbury.

These two parks are linked by the Paugussett and Pomperaug Trails. Both are on the Housatonic River, Kettletown bordering for two miles on an impoundment called Lake Zoar.

Camping: 80 sites at Kettletown.
Fishing/Swimming: Available.

Boating: Ramp at Indian Well.

For further information contact: Office of State Parks and Recreation, 165 Capitol Ave., Hartford, CT 06106. ☎ (203) 566-2304.

Macedonia Brook State Park

Location: 4 miles north of Keny on SR 341.

*T*he site is mostly forested with mixed hardwoods. Woodland bird species are abundant during migrations, and birders often camp so they can be in the woods at dawn.

Camping: 84 sites.
Hiking/Backpacking: The Appalachian Trail traverses the Park, crossing Cobble Mountain and Pine Hill. Other trails are color-coded.
Camping: Two lean-tos.
Fishing: Trout are stocked.

For further information contact: Office of State Parks and Recreation, 165 Capitol Ave., Hartford, CT 06106. ☎ (203) 566-2304.

Mansfield Hunting Area/Mansfield Hollow State Park

Location: South of Storrs on Route 195.

*T*he developed area of the Park is on a wooded bluff overlooking the lake. Swimming is not permitted (the lake is a public water supply), but picnicking, boating, and fishing are allowed. The lake is deep enough for boating. The area is largely mixed hardwood forest, with reverting fields, brushy marsh, and beaver flowages. Wildlife is abundant.

Hiking: Easy trails run along the shoreline and through fields and forest. A spur extends to the Nipmuck Trail.
Hunting: Pheasant, grouse, quail, and small game.
Fishing: Said to be one of the state's best areas for trout, smallmouth bass, bullhead, and chain pickerel.
Boating: Paved launching ramp. No hp limit.

For further information contact: Office of State Parks and Recreation, 165 Capitol Ave., Hartford, CT 06106. ☎ (203) 566-2304, Wildlife Bureau, ☎ (203) 566-4683.

Mashamoquet Brook State Park

Location: 5 miles southwest of Putnam on SR 44.

This park in the eastern highlands is always filled on weekends. Rolling woodlands can be seen in all stages of succession: reverting fields, stands of smooth alder, juniper, and young red cedar; birch replacing cedar; oak replacing birch. The swamp has a short boardwalk. Large stone formations are found in the Park.

Camping: Two campgrounds, with a total of 55 sites.
Hiking: Short trails within the Park.

For further information contact: Office of State Parks and Recreation, 165 Capitol Ave., Hartford, CT 06106. ☎ (203) 566-2304.

Meshomasic State Forest

Location: North of SR 66 at Cobalt.

Hiking: The Shenipsit Trail extends north through the Meshomasic and Shenipsit State Forests to the Massachusetts border.
Hunting/Fishing: Deer and small game. Trout are stocked.
Ski touring: Trails and unplowed roads.

For further information contact: Office of State Parks and Recreation, 165 Capitol Ave., Hartford, CT 06106. ☎ (203) 566-2304.

Mohawk State Forest

Location: West of Torrington, about 10 miles on SR 4.

The 35-mile Mattatuck Trail crosses the north end of this State Forest (as did the Appalachian Trail until it was relocated due to complaints from local residents).

Black Spruce Bog, near Forest Headquarters has a trail and board-walk. Pitcherplant, sundew, mountain holly, and other bog species can be found here.

Great Gulf Trail is a one-mile loop just east of the Toumey Road entrance.

For further information contact: Office of State Parks and Recreation, 165 Capitol Ave., Hartford, CT 06106. ☎ (203) 566-2304.

Nassahegon State Forest

Location: Just outside of Burlington on SR 4.

This odd-shaped Forest is of interest chiefly as a link in the Tunxis Trail, with several blazed local trails permitting loop hikes.

For further information contact: Office of State Parks and Recreation, 165 Capitol Ave., Hartford, CT 06106. ☎ (203) 566-2304.

Natchaug State Forest

Location: 4 miles south of Phoenixville on SR 198.

Natchaug, meaning "land between the rivers," is one of the largest State Forests. Most of the Forest is just east of the Natchaug River.

Natchaug State Forest is a hiker's paradise and one of the few where backpacking is allowed. Camping by permit is also allowed at designated sites. The Nipmuck Trail extends about 26 miles north from Mansfield Hollow State Park to SR 171 in Union, near the Bigelow Hollow State Park.

Hiking/ Backpacking: About 55 miles of trails.
Horse riding: Trails and roads. A horse camp has 28 sites; reservations required.
Hunting: Deer, cottontail, squirrel, raccoon, grouse, woodcock, pheasant, and waterfowl.
Fishing: Trout stocked. The Natchaug River and other streams may also be fished.
Ski touring: Unplowed roads and trails.

For further information contact: Office of State Parks and Recreation, 165 Capitol Ave., Hartford, CT 06106. ☎ (203) 566-2304.

Nehantic State Forest

Location: From the Connecticut Turnpike, head north on SR 156.

*B*elieve it or not, the forest is still recovering from heavy damage in a 1938 hurricane and offers only a limited, mixed variety of hardwoods, small streams, marshes, and reverting fields.

Hiking: Trails throughout the area, used chiefly by hunters.
Hunting: Grouse, deer, squirrel, and cottontail.
Fishing: The ponds offer warmwater species.

For further information contact: Office of State Parks and Recreation, 165 Capitol Ave., Hartford, CT 06106. ☎ (203) 566-2304.

Nepaug State Forest

Location: North of US 202 just north of Old Lyme.

*B*esides occasional hunting, the Forest serves mainly as a link on the Tunxis Trail. The Trail runs west along US 202.

For further information contact: Office of State Parks and Recreation, 165 Capitol Ave., Hartford, CT 06106. ☎ (203) 566-2304.

Nipmuck State Forest

Location: On the NE CT/MA border.
From I-86, exit 105 NW on SR 190 for 4½ miles.

*M*orey Pond is in a forest setting. Bear Den Marsh and Sessions Meadow Marsh are waterfowl areas.

Hiking: The Nipmuck Trail has two southern branches, both originating near Mansfield Center. They soon join and continue north through Bigelow Hollow State Park into the Nipmuck State Forest, through Bigelow Hollow State Park into the Nipmuck State Forest, about 25 miles. Another trail links the Forest with the Natchaug Trail. There are other trails and woods roads to hike.

Hunting: Grouse, squirrel, snowshoe hare, deer, woodcock, and raccoon.

Fishing: Trout stocked in ponds and streams.

Boating: Ramp on Morey Pond.

Ski touring: Trails and unplowed roads.

For more information, contact: Office of State Parks and Recreation, 165 Capitol Ave., Hartford, CT 06106. ☎ (203) 566-2304.

Pachaug State Forest

Location: SE of Plainfield on SR 49.

The Pachaug State Forest has several streams, seven lakes, numerous impoundments, open and brushy marshes, and white-cedar swamps.

The Pachaug is one of the few Connecticut forests with campgrounds and where backpacking is permitted. Overnight hikers must have permits and use designated shelters.

Green Falls, off SR 138, three miles east of Voluntown, has only 18 campsites. It is chiefly a day-use area, often crowded in fine weather because it offers swimming and boating as well as fishing. Parking is limited.

H. H. Chapman Area is about one mile north of Voluntown off SR 49. This area includes the Pachaug State Forest Headquarters, Beachdale Pond, and a boat launch site on the Pachaug River.

Great Meadow complex is due east of SR 49, north of the river. It has a 70-acre wildlife marsh, oak forest, hardwood swamps, hemlock stands, white pine plantations, and open fields.

Hell Hollow-Sue Hopkins Area, off SR 49 east of Ekonk, has a good variety of wildlife.

Camping: Two campgrounds with a total of 40 sites.

Hiking/Backpacking: On the Nehantic, Quinebaug and Pachaug trails. The Pachaug Trail extends for 30 miles from Green Falls Pond to Pachaug Pond. The Nehantic Trail, about 14 miles, runs from Green Falls Pond to Hopeville Pond. Quinebaugh is a 5½-mile trail linked with the Pachaug.

Horse riding: Trails are open to horse travel, and woods roads are also suitable.

Hunting: Deer, squirrel, cottontail, raccoon, grouse, pheasant, duck, fox, and woodcock.

Fishing: Seven lakes and nine impoundments.

Canoeing: The Pachaug River and a number of lakes.

Ski touring: Trails and unplowed roads.

For further information contact: Office of State Parks and Recreation, 165 Capitol Ave., Hartford, CT 06106. ☎ (203) 566-2304.

Penwood State Park/Talcott Mountain State Park

Location: 3 miles west of Bloomfield on SR 185.

Penwood was given to the State in 1944; the donor required that it be left in natural condition. He and his wife had built many of the trails, as well as a road artfully designed to fit into the mountain contours, passing a high pond. The highest elevation is 741 ft.

Hiking: Slopes are moderate to steep, forested, with rock outcrops. Seasonal wildflowers include Dutchman's-breeches, trillium, bloodroot, hepatica, trailing arbutus, trout lily, and wood anemone. Common birds here include turkey vulture, bald eagle, and pileated woodpecker.

For further information contact: Office of State Parks and Recreation, 165 Capitol Ave., Hartford, CT 06106. ☎ (203) 566-2304.

Peoples State Forest

Location: From Winsted, east on US 44.

This forest was acquired in 1923 thanks to the Connecticut Forest and Park Association. The Matthies Grove Area, about a mile north of SR 318, has a large car park, a ball field, many picnic tables, and other facilities. Nearby is a grove of 200-year-old white pines. This is a wonderful recreation spot for local residents.

Hiking/Backpacking: Trails with four Adirondack shelters for overnighting.
Camping: 30 sites.
Hunting: Grouse, cottontail, snowshoe hare, deer, squirrel, raccoon, and some waterfowl.
Fishing: River (trout stocked).

For further information contact: Office of State Parks and Recreation, 165 Capitol Ave., Hartford, CT 06106. ☎ (203) 566-2304.

Quaddick State Forest & State Park

Location: Northeast corner of the state. From US 395, exit 99.

The chief attraction here is Quaddick Reservoir, over two miles long. The Park attracts visitors for swimming and sailing. The forest, north of the Park, has hiking opportunities.

For further information contact: Office of State Parks and Recreation, 165 Capitol Ave., Hartford, CT 06106. ☎ (203) 566-2304.

Rocky Neck State Park

Location: From Connecticut Turnpike take Exit 72, then south.

This State Park is always crowded during the late spring and summer months. It is one of Connecticut's few state beaches. Out of season it is delightful and its several habitats provide interest for birders.

Camping: 169 sites.
Hiking: About four miles of wonderfully kept trails.
Fishing: Mackerel, striped bass, blackfish and flounder.

For further information contact: Office of State Parks and Recreation, 165 Capitol Ave., Hartford, CT 06106. ☎ (203) 566-2304.

Roy & Margot Larsen Sanctuary

Location: From Merritt Parkway, use Exit 44.

The purpose of this sanctuary is environmental education. An illustrated guide to the 6½ miles of trails explains in great detail what visitors see and makes it easy for all to understand. The Society sponsors educational nature programs for adults and children. A recent addition is a trail for handicapped visitors.

No pets, horses, or picnicking.

For further information contact: Connecticut Audubon Society, 2325 Burr St., Fairfield, CT 06430. ☎ (203) 259-6305.

Salmon River State Forest

Location: Along the Salmon River.

Hiking: The Salmon River Trail has two loops, both originating at Day Pond. The Forest also has hiking opportunities on unmanned wood roads.
Fishing: The Salmon has excellent trout fishing, including a fly-fishing-only section.
Canoeing/Kayaking: Popular in early spring. It's about five miles to the Connecticut River.

For further information contact: Office of State Parks and Recreation, 165 Capitol Ave., Hartford, CT 06106. ☎ (203) 566-2304.

Salt Meadow National Wildlife Refuge

Location: From I-95 near Clifton, take Exit 64 and head south for ½ mile and make a left on Clifton Rd.

This site is near the coast but as much as 110 ft. above sea level. Unfortunately, the Penn Central Railroad divides the area and does take a little something away from its beauty. Prominent tree species are oaks, yellow poplar, and black cherry.

Birds: Over 200 species recorded. Osprey nest on a platform in the marsh.

Hiking: Three miles of trails begin at the entrance parking lot.

For further information contact: Ninigret National Wildlife Refuge Complex, Box 307, Charlestown, RI 02813. ☎ (401) 364-9124.

Satan's Kingdom State Recreation Area

Location: On US 44 just south of New Hartford.

*E*ven though Satan's Kingdom is called a state recreation area, it's commercially operated. The only activity is tubing – floating in large tubes down the Farmington River for about two hours. The concessionaire provides tubes, other gear, and a shuttle bus.

For more information contact: North American Canoe Tours, 65 Black Point Rd., Niantic, CT 06357. ☎ (203) 693-6465.

Sleeping Giant State Park

Location: 2 miles north of Hamden n SR 10.

A 30-mile trail network winds through mixed hardwood forest with mountain laurel, brooks, and swamps. Highest point is 739 ft. on Mt. Carmel, providing a view of Long Island Sound. Very well marked, complete with beautifully written and entertaining trail signs.

Camping: Beware! There are only eight campsites in this park and they are always in use. Camping here is not advised because of lack of space.

Hiking: The Quinnipiac Trail, oldest in the blue-blazed hiking trails system, 21 miles long, passes over the Giant.

For further information contact: Office of State Parks and Recreation, 165 Capitol Ave., Hartford, CT 06106. ☎ (203) 566-2304.

Tunxis State Forest

Location: Right on the Connecticut/Massachusetts border – crossed by SR 20.

*W*hat wonderful hiking! Be sure to take the well-marked Tunxis Trail due north from its crossing on SR 219 east of the reservoir. The area is gently rolling, somewhat challenging for novice hikers – most of it between 1,000 and 1,160 ft. elevation.

Habitats include reverting fields, ponds, brooks and swamps, beaver flowages, and forest. Hike through an open mixed hardwood forest and, on a slight rise, enter an extensive dark grove of hemlock. On the higher ground of Pine Mountain are moosewood, hobblebush, mountain ash, and wood sorrel.

Howells Pond is popular with fishermen. From West Hartland, proceed NW on West St. The roads don't match those on the forest map, but the pond will be found easily.

Hiking: The Tunxis Trail is the most popular route. Use of trail bikes is not advisable.
Hunting: Grouse, cottontail, snowshoe hare, gray squirrel, raccoon, wild turkey, some waterfowl.

For further information contact: Office of State Parks and Recreation, 165 Capitol Ave., Hartford, CT 06106. ☎ (203) 566-2304.

White Memorial Conservation Center

Location: Starting at Litchfield head 2.2 miles west on US 202.

*T*he Foundation owns and maintains this extensive preserve for conservation, education, recreation, and research. It has 60% of the shoreline of Bantam Lake, the largest natural lake in Connecticut at 2.4 miles long.

Plants: About 60% of the area is forested with mixed hardwoods, white pine, and spruce. The understory includes mountain laurel, azalea, and shadbush. Many wildflowers, ferns, and mosses, and wetland species.
Birds: Checklist available includes waterfowl, rails, herons, gulls, terns, hawks, owls, and numerous songbirds.

Mammals: Common species include deer, beaver, cottontail, chipmunk, squirrel, raccoon. Less often seen: mink, weasel, bobcat, flying squirrel, and fox.

Camping: Two campgrounds, 48 and 20 sites.

Hiking: About 25 miles of woodland roads, 10 miles of marked trails. Trails include a section of the Mattatuck Trail, a major trail connecting with the Appalachian Trail.

Fishing: Bantam Lake. Northern pike, bass.

Swimming: Beach on Bantam Lake.

Boating: Marina opposite the Folly Point Campground has ramp and moorings.

Ski touring: Trails and woodland roads.

For further information contact: Headquarters, Route 202, Litchfield, CT 06759. Business office: ☎ (203) 567-0857. Conservation Center: ☎ (203) 567-0015.

Historic Sites

Weir Farm National Historic Site

Directions to the Weir Farm National Historic Site from the New York area:

From the Tappan Zee Bridge:
Follow 287 East to 684 North.
Follow 684 to Katonah, New York.
Take Route 35 East to Ridgefield, Connecticut.
At the fountain, turn left onto Main Street.
Turn right onto Route 102 East.
Turn right onto Old Branchville Road (landmark – sign for Nutmeg Ridge on left).
At STOP turn right onto Nod Hill Road.
Weir Farm NHS is .7 miles from stop on the right side.

Following I-95 North into Connecticut:
Take exit 15 for Route 7 North and follow to Branchville.
In Branchville turn left onto Route 102 West.
Take second left onto Old Branchville Road.
At STOP turn left onto Nod Hill Road.
Weir Farm NHS is .7 miles from stop on the right side.

$\mathcal{F}$or more than 100 years Weir Farm has been an inspirational focal point to many generations of artists. At few other places is an American landscape so intimately tied to the paintings, drawings, etchings and other works of art produced there.

The American Impressionist painter Julian Alden Weir (1852-1919) purchased this Branchville, Connecticut farm in 1882. The property included 153 acres, which Weir eventually expanded to 238 acres. The "quiet, plain, little house among the rocks" held special appeal for the painter. For forty years, Weir made this his summer studio and home to his family. He built a painting studio, twice enlarged the house, and continuously worked the landscape, adding and massaging features to suit his highly discerning eye. The farm became, in a sense, a big sprawling palette – its buildings, stone walls, woods, and gardens all elements in the painter's evolving composition. It also inspired subject matter for much of Weir's work and offered countless excursions, both recreational and creative, to his wide circle of friends that included the painters Albert Pinkham Ryder, John Twachtman, and Childe Hassam. These were regular visitors to Branchville. Known for generosity of spirit, as well as the legacy of his professional life as an artist, Weir recognized early the importance of a creative center – a focal point – for both life and art. "Home is the starting place," Weir wrote to his future wife in anticipation of their marriage and move to Brachville.

In 1931, the sculptor Mahonri Young married J. Alden Weir's daughter Dorothy and came to live at the farm. A grandson of Brigham Young, Mahonri Young was already recognized for his small studies in bronze of the common working man. The studio he built at Branchville, consequently, was custom-designed to accommodate his monumental public work. A person of great creative versatility, Young worked in many artistic media and, in time, set up an etching room off the sculpture studio. Dorothy Weir Young was also an accomplished artist in both oils and watercolor. She trained at her father's side and took over his Branchville studio following his death.

Since Mahonri Young's death in 1957, the cultivation of both art and life at Weir Farms has been carried on by the artists Sperry and Doris Andrews. The artists recognized this as a place of extraordinary significance to American art and were instrumental in preserving the landscape and its artistic legacy for the visiting public and future generations of artists.

Weir Farm National Historic Site

N

to other trails

to routes 7 and 12

Site boundary
Stone walls
Footpaths
Open to public on guided tours only

to other trails

Nod Hill Road

Weir Farm Lane

Pond

1
2
5 4
3

Pelham Lane

6
7

to Weir Preserve

1. Ice House/Chicken Coop
2. Weir Barn
3. Weir House
4. Weir Studio
5. Young Studio
6. Burlington House Visitor Center
7. Burlingham Barn

Weir Farm was established as a National Historic Site in 1990 and planning is now under way to provide a full range of opportunities for visitors.

The Visitor Center, located in the Burlingham House, features an introduction to the site and changing art exhibitions. Scheduled tours are available of J. Alden Weir's studio. Special exhibitions, lectures, art workshops and a visiting artist program are offered by the Weir Farm Heritage Trust, a nonprofit partner with the National Park Service.

Encroaching development motivated Weir Farm's preservation. In 1985, a group of neighbors and concerned citizens who would not accept the loss of Wier Pond and the farm to suburban development enlisted the help of the Trust for Public Land (TPL), a national land conservation organization dedicated to preserving important natural, cultural, and historical resources for public use. TPL took the initiative in protecting the land by temporarily purchasing key acreage until a permanent management agency could be identified. In 1989, members of the group that initially sought TPL's intervention formed the Weir Farm Heritage Trust, the source of grass-roots support for preserving the property. In 1992 and 1993, TPL and the Connecticut Department of Environmental Protection, which provided the primary financing for the project, transferred the property to the National Park Service.

Weir Farms NHS embraces 57 of the 238 acres J. Alden Weir purchased in Branchville between 1882 and 1907. It includes his home, studio, barn, and outbuildings, all listed on the National Register of Historic Places. There are also woodlands, wetlands, and the pond he built in 1896 with prize money from the Boston Art Club. The former Foster Webb Farm, occupied between 1931 and 1980 by his daughter, Cora Weir Burlingham is included as well. An enterprising avocational farmer, Weir maintained an orchard and a vegetable garden, raised grains and grasses, kept livestock, and planted specimen trees in open fields to provide shade for his cows.

Weir's house, studio, and grounds are remarkably little changed since he used them a century ago. The farm has not been built upon since the sculptor Mahonri Young, who married Weir's daughter, Dorothy, in 1932, completed his studio in 1934. Barns and shed, fieldstone walls and hedgerows, and vestiges of orchards and grain fields remain today not only as testiment to the site's agrarian heritage but as highly suggestive reminders of the effect the farm had, and continues to have, on artists.

Connecticut Impressionist Art Trail

Childe Hassam. Theodore Robinson, J. Alden Weir. John Twacht-mann. Nearly one hundred years ago, these artists and other like them – perhaps like you today – were attracted to Connecticut for its beauty and charm.

They brought with them world-class training, extraordinary talent, and a rare appreciation for the stirring landscapes that are Connecticut's alone. Some stayed and some did not, but the very best helped to create on canvas (and in some cases on door panels and walls) what has become known around the world as American Impressionism.

Now American Impressionism can be seen in a way that dramatically heightens both appreciation and enjoyment. When you set out on the Connecticut Impressionist Art Trail, you will experience more than a guided visit to 11 museums boasting some of the finest American Impressionism in the world. You will also discover the places where it all was born – a countryside whose beauty still inspires and a country life whose simplicity still renews.

Bruce Museum

From the West, your first stop on the Impressionist Art Trail is the Bruce Museum. Just off I-95's exit 3, the Bruce is near Greenwich's four-star restaurants, hotels, and shops.

Recently expanded and renovated with extensive art, natural science exhibitions and collection displays, the Bruce Museum today is a spacious, contemporary facility starring an impressive collection of works by Childe Hassam, Leonard Ochtman, and Emil Carlsen – all artists who painted in the Cos Cob/Greenwich area – a location of critical importance to the development of the American Impressionist movement.

Bush-Holly House

*M*inutes from the Bruce lies a classic 1732 saltbox, the Bush-Holley House, alongside Strickland Brook in Cos Cob. At this charming, unassuming home, now a National Historic Landmark, you can witness first-hand the evidence of camaraderie shared by the artists who gathered here in the 1890's. Childe Hassam, John Twachtman, Theodore Robinson, Elmer Livingston MacRae, and others painted the local scenery, told lively stories, played charades and popped corn in the fireplace. In addition to offering you a sense of this American Impressionist colony and the stunning work its artists produced, the Bush-Holley House also presents a spectacular collection of 18th-century furnishings and accessories.

Florence Griswold Museum

*A*bout 35 minutes from New Haven on I-95 North is Lyme, a return to rural simplicity. Home of the famous Lyme art colony, this area was first described by colony founder Henry Ward Ranger as a setting "only waiting to be painted." At the Florence Griswold Museum, with six landscaped acres, beautiful gardens, and the recently restored studio of artist William Chadwick, Ranger's words still ring true. "Miss Florence's" boarding house, now a National Historic Landmark, housed such artists as Childe Hassam, Willard Metcalf, Will Howe Foote, Matilda Browne and Charles Eber, all of whom are well represented in the museum's permanent collection. In addition to historic period settings, don't miss the famed dining room, lined with over 30 panels painted by the boarding artists.

Hartford Steam Boiler Inspection & Insurance Co.

*N*o tour of American Impressionism in Connecticut could be complete without seeing the display on the executive floor of the Hartford Steam Boiler Inspection and Insurance Company in downtown Hartford. Over 100 American impressionist works are included in this collection, which consists of early 18th- through early 20th-century Connecticut paintings and furniture. Especially notable are works of artists from Old Lyme and Cos Cob: Henry Ward Ranger, Willard Metcalf, Edward Rook, Guy Wiggins and the most eminent Childe Hassam from the Lyme colony; and the celebrated John Twachtman, Theodore Robinson and J. Alden Weir from Cos Cob. Since this gallery is open by appointment only, call ahead.

Hill-Stead Museum

The Hill-Stead Museum, in Farmington, offers you a glimpse behind American Impressionism. As at the Yale Gallery, the Hill-Stead pays tribute to the powerful influence the French Impressionists exerted on this American phenomenon, with important paintings by Monet, Manet, and Degas handsomely displayed in a domestic setting, just as the artists intended. In addition to the permanent collection of art and furnishings, the Hill-Stead is notable for its architecture. The house, a National Historic Landmark, was built in 1901 by industrialist Alfred Atmore Pope and is a unique collaboration between his daughter Theodate and the firm of McKim, Mead and White. A restored sunken garden complements the house, while a sweeping hill-top view and splendid fields and orchards also await you.

Lyman Allyn Art Museum

Connecticut Impressionism is well represented at the Lyman Allyn Art Museum, which is housed in an imposing Neo-Classical building overlooking the US Coast Guard Academy. Here, paintings by Willard Metcalf, William Chadwick, and other members of the Mystic and Old Lyme art colonies are displayed along with important works from the Tonalist and Hudson River schools that led into Impressionism. The Museum, named for a 19th-century New London sea captain, also features an impressive range of American, African, and Asian decorative and fold arts, as well as a collection of antique dolls and miniatures.

New Britain Museum of American Art

Twenty minutes away from Hartford at the New Britain Museum of American Art, the visitor can experience an entire survey of our nation's art history from John Singleton Copley to Sol Lewitt. Established in 1903, the museum houses over 4,000 works. The collection is especially rich for the American Impressionist trailblazers. Mary Cassatt, William Merritt Chase, Theodore Robinson, Childe Hassam, John Henry Twatchman, Julian Alden Weir, Willard Metcalf, Frank Benson, Frederick Frieseke, Richard Miller, Arthur Clifton Goodwin, Ernest Lawson, Maurice Prendergast, and Guy Wiggins are all well represented.

Wadsworth Atheneum

Hartford's Wadsworth Atheneum, founded in 1842 by Daniel Wadsworth, is not only one of America's premier museums, it is also the country's oldest continuously operating public art museum. Just a block away from the Hartford Steam Boiler Collection, the Atheneum's American Impressionist collection includes Childe Hassam, John Twachtman, Thomas Dewing, and William Merritt Chase. The Atheneum's collections, which span more than 5,000 years of art history, also include Renaissance and Baroque paintings, European and American decorative arts, ceramics and textiles, 19th-century American and European landscapes, and 20th-century masterpieces.

Weir Farm National Historic Site

Just up Route 7, in Connecticut's only national park, is the Weir Farm National Historic Site. Weir Farm was the earliest center of American Impressionist activity in Connecticut and still offers visitors an immersion into the landscapes that inspired the artists. Home to J. Alden Weir (1852-1919) for nearly 40 years, the farm hosted many artists including Childe Hassam, John Twachtman, Albert Pinkham Ryder and John Singer Sargent. Today, you can enjoy self-guided tours to revisit the same vistas painted by these artists – landscapes little changed from those times. In addition, a visitor center offers orientation, changing exhibits, tours to J. Alden Weir's studio and special programs to keep the site's artistic legacy alive.

William Benton Museum of Art

$\mathcal{A}$t the center of the University of Connecticut's scenic campus in Storrs, the William Benton Museum of Art proudly displays a delightful sampling of American Impressionist works by Emil Carlsen, Mary Cassatt and J. Alden Weir. While these works reveal what depth of talent the American Impressionist movement attracted, the Benton is also worthwhile for its engaging collection of Tiffany lamps and other American art and artifacts. In fact, since the museum's inception in 1966, its collections have expanded ten-fold. Before making this remarkably scenic trip, be sure the museum is open, since the Benton has an academic calendar.

Yale University Art Gallery

$\mathcal{H}$ere, on the historic Yale campus in New Haven, you can trace the beginnings of the Impressionist movement with paintings by Monet, Renoir, Pissarro, Degas and Sisley, before moving into the American Galleries. Here, in one of the world's finest collections of American paintings and decorative arts, the work of Impressionist artists Childe Hassam and John Twachtman complement master works by their contemporaries, Thomas Eakins, Winslow Homer, George Bellows and Edward Hopper. Founded in 1832, when the artist patriot John Trumbull gave 100 paintings to Yale, the Art Gallery's encyclopedic collections have now grown to well over 100,000 objects from every period in art, from ancient Egyptian times to the present.

For further information contact: Connecticut Impressionist Art Trail, PO Box 793, Old Lyme, CT 06371.

Maine

State Parks & Historic Sites

Campground Reservations

Campsite reservations are offered at 11 State Park campgrounds. Reservations may be made by phone with Visa or Mastercard ☎ (800) 332-1501 (in state) or (207) 287-3824, Mon-Fri, 9 am until 3 pm; or, by mail using check, money order, or credit card. Send requests to: Reservation Clerk Parks and Recreation, Station 22, Augusta, ME 04333.

Reservations must be made in the year for which they are to be used. It is necessary to make reservations two weeks in advance of the first night stay. The reservation period is from June 15th through Labor Day. Mail-in reservation request forms are available and may be obtained at the Augusta office (address above). Reservations will be accepted from the first working day in January through the third Friday in August.

Note: Absolutey NO state park campgrounds offer water or electrical hookups. Some areas have dumping stations.

Arnold Trail State Historic Site

Location: This trail stretches from Fort Popham, at the mouth of the Kennebec River, north and west to the Canadian border at Coburn Gore.

The trail traces the route followed by Colonel Benedict Arnold and his troops in the autumn of 1775 on the Maine portion of their historic march to Quebec. Some of the buildings passed by Arnold's men are still standing today, including Fort Western in Augusta, Fort Halifax in Winslow, and the old Pownalborough Courthouse in Dresden.

For further information contact: Arnold Trail State Historic Site, Center Hill, RR 1, Box 610, Weld, ME 04285. ☎ (207) 585-2261.

Aroostook State Park

Location: On Echo Lake, off US 1 south of Presque Isle.

Facilities in this state park include 30 campsites, a picnic area, boat launch, bathhouse, beach (lifeguard provided in season), and an information station. Camping, swimming, boating, fishing, snowmobiling, cross-country skiing, and hiking are just a few of the activities offered.

The four-mile cross-country ski trail doubles as a hiking trail in the summer. All park boundaries are marked and highly visible. The park encompasses Quaggy Jo Mountain and Echo Lake, providing year-round activities. Quaggy Jo Mountain offers a geological past. Underlying limestone formations prove the presence of an ancient sea, and the mountain's outer surface suggests volcanic lava flow from an unknown origin. Quaggy Jo is the shortened form of the Indian name "QuaQuaJo," which translates to "twin peaked." A variety of animals and birds live here in the mixed forest. Squirrels, chipmunks, raccoons, and skunks are most frequently seen, but there are also white-tailed deer, moose, bobcat, foxes, coyotes, and black bears. Alert watchers may see many types of birds, including owls, ruffed grouse, shore birds, and a host of songbirds.

The oldest park in the Maine park system, Aroostook originated in 1939 with 100 acres and has grown to today's 650 acres. Situated at the base of Quaggy Jo Mountain, it offers visitors over 20 miles of hiking rails with great views of the surrounding area. In the winter, these same trails provide 14 miles of groomed cross-country ski trails.

For further information contact: Aroostook State Park, 87 State Park Rd., Presque Isle, ME 04769. ☎ (207) 768-8341.

Birch Point Beach State Park

Location: On Birch Point in Owl's Head. Take State Route 73 south from Rockland. Turn left on North Shore Drive, then right on the Knox County Airport road. Drive past the airport and take the first right.

*A*ctivities include salt water fishing from the rocky shore or sand beach and picnicking on the beach or on picnic tables provided. No charcoal grills have been installed and no fires are allowed at this area.

Birch Point Beach State Park provides scenic access to the shores of Penobscot Bay, with views of the Muscle Ridge Islands. Climb on the rocks or stroll along a beautiful sand beach. The crescent-shaped beach provides opportunities for swimming in gentle surf. There is no lifeguard on duty and no regular staff, phone, or equipment to provide assistance in emergency situations.

For further information contact: Birch Point Beach State Park, RR 1, Box 1070, Thomaston, ME 04861. ☎ (207) 596-2253.

Bradbury Mountain State Park

Location: 5 miles from the Freeport-Durham exit off US 95.

*F*acilities in Bradbury Mountain State Park include several campsites, a ballfield, trails, and picnic area.

Hiking/cross-country skiing trails through wooded terrain are available, with several leading to the top of 460-foot Bradbury Mountain, providing a view of Casco Bay and surrounding countryside.

For further information contact: Bradbury Mountain State Park, Hallowell Rd., Pownal, ME 04069. ☎ (207) 688-4712.

Camden Hills State Park

Location: 2 miles north of Camden on US Route 1.

Brochures: Park brochures available to the public include a park trails map, a park campsite map, a park brochure, and a Mt. Battie history handout.

Camping: 112 sites are available for family camping. Reservations available after January 1 through the State Park Reservation System. For group camping, see "group" below.

Cross-Country Skiing: Although trails are not groomed for cross-country skiing at the park, many visitors use park trails and the Mt. Battie Road for skiing during winter months. Recorded snow conditions report for the park is available 24 hours a day at ☎ (207) 236-3109. Maintained cross-country ski trails are available at nearby Camp Tanglewood, a leased facility on park lands.

Firewood: Campfire wood is for sale at the campground Welcome Station.

Group Area with Shelter: A reservable group area with a shelter is available at the picnic area. The group shelter accommodates up to 50 people comfortably, and is available for reserved use between May 15 and October 15. The shelter reservation fee is $50. Reservations can be made after January 1 by contracting the park office.

Group Camping: Five group sites are located in the picnic area. Each site can accommodate up to 12 people. Groups up to 60 people can reserve one or more sites. Group reservation fee is $10 per group. Reservations can be made after January 1 by contacting the park office.

Hiking: 22 miles of hiking are available over 17 trails, with access from five major trail heads. Trail maps are available at the Welcome Station. NOTE: Trails are open for use throughout the year. Parking and toilet facilities are maintained throughout the year at the campground trail head.

Hunting/Fur Trapping: Hunting and trapping are allowed in certain sections of the park from October 1 to April 30 as prescribed by the laws of the Maine Department of Inland Fisheries and Wildlife. Maps indicating sections of the park closed to hunting and trapping will be posted at trail heads and bulletin boards during the November open season on white-tail deer. Fur trappers are required to obtain written permission from the park manager before trapping on park property.

Mountain Biking: Approximately five miles of trails are designated as multi-use, with bicycling allowed.

Mt. Battie Auto Road: Visitors may drive or hike to the summit of Mt. Battie for an excellent view of Camden Harbor, Penobscot Bay, and inland lakes and rivers. An observation tower, binoculars, and interpretive panels are available at the summit. A "Mt. Battie Pass" is available, allowing five vehicle trips up the Auto Road. An informational brochure is available at the Welcome Station.

Pay Phones: Available at the campground Welcome Station.

Picnicking: Picnic tables and charcoal grills are available at the picnic area. Level access sites are available, but toilet facilities may be difficult for people with mobility problems.

Playground: Playground facilities at the picnic area.

Rock Climbing: Rock climbing is allowed within the park in accordance with Bureau policies. Contact the park office for more information.

Shore Access: Trails from the picnic area lead to the shores of Penobscot Bay.

Showers: Hot showers are available at the family campground (May 15 - October 15).

Snowmobiling: Locally maintained snowmobile trails (approximately eight miles) run across the park lands.

Toilet Facilities: Flush toilets are available at the picnic area and at the family and group campgrounds. Vault toilets are located at the Mt. Battie Summit and at the campground trail head.

Trailer Sanitary Station: A dump station is available for self-contained camping units at the family campground. There is a $5 fee per unit.

Watchable Wildlife: In addition to wildlife common at most State Parks, Camden Hills offers opportunities to watch hawk migrations in the spring and fall, and to see turkey vultures circling in the sky.

Water: Drinking water is available at the family and group campgrounds, the picnic area, and the Campground Trail Head (May 15 through October 15).

Weddings: Weddings can be arranged at the summit of Mt. Battie. Only one wedding party is allowed on the summit at any one time. A maximum of 75 people are allowed per wedding party because of limited available parking. Contact the park office for information concerning outdoor weddings in the park.

Special Events & Activities

Stargazing Program: Stargazing/astronomy programs are available for family and organized group camping parties during the camping season by appointment only. This program is provided free by a local volunteer. Contact the park office for more information.

Guided Trail Hikes: A guided trail hike is available for individuals or small groups on most weekends from May 1 to November 1. This free service is provided by a local volunteer, by appointment only. Contact the park office for more information.

Christmas Star: A giant Christmas Star, sponsored by the Camden Rotary, is lighted nightly on the Mt. Battie Tower between November 24 and January 1.

For further information contact: Camden Hills State Park, HCR 60, Box 3110, Camden, ME 04843. ☎ (207) 236-0849. Park Office: ☎ (207) 236-3109. Welcome Station: ☎ (207) 236-4214.

Cobscook Bay State Park

Location: Located 5 miles south of Dennysville on US 1.

Cobscook is an Indian name meaning boiling tide, an apt description of the action of the 24-foot tidal currents in the bay. Located near Quoddy Head State Park, Moosehorn National Wildlife Refuge, and Franklin D. Roosevelt International Park on Campobello Island in New Brunswick.

Facilities: Campsites, scenic road, picnic area, boat launch, showers, firewood available.

Activities: Camping, boating, fishing, cross-country skiing, hiking, bird watching, designated Watchable Wildlife Area.

For further information contact: Cobscook Bay State Park, RR 1, Box 51, Dennysville, ME 04628. ☎ (207) 726-4412.

Colonial Pemaquid State Historic Site

*Location: 1½ miles off Route 130 in Bristol, situated on the east side of
Pemaquid Harbor near Pemaquid Beach.*

Archaeological Excavations: Extensive archaeological excavations
have unearthed 14 foundations of 17th- and 18th-century village
structures and officers' quarters of Forts William Henry and
Frederick. These findings and accompanying interpretive panels
are available for public view.

Boat Access Facility: A hard surface tidal boat launch ramp, with
parking, is available on park grounds.

Brochures: A general park brochure is available. A museum guide
may be borrowed for self-guided museum tours.

Cemetery: A historic private cemetery is open to the public on park
grounds.

Fishing: Salt water fishing is enjoyed by visitors from the park's
pier or along the water's edge.

Fort Frederick: Excavated ruins of Fort Frederick (1729 - 1759) are
interpreted at the park. The fort was abandoned in 1759.

Fort House: Constructed in the early 1970s on the grounds of
Colonial Pemaquid, the Fort House is used primarily for artifact
storage and archaeological research. The building is not presently
open to the public.

Fort William Henry: Fort William Henry was constructed in 1692,
and was destroyed by French and Indian raiders in 1696. A replica
of the Fort William Henry tower was built by the state of Maine in
1908. This tower is open today and contains exhibits of the area's
history.

Friends of Colonial Pemaquid: Organized in 1993, the Friends
work to support the operations of Colonial Pemaquid State Historic Site. For more information contact Friends through: Mrs.
Phillip Crocker, HC 62, Box 95, New Harbor, ME 04554. ☎ (207)
677-3618.

Groups and Group Tours: Tours and interpretive programs are
available for groups by reservation from May 15 to October 21.
Groups up to 100 people may be given tours in shifts. School and
children's groups should be chaperoned by at least three adults for
every 25 children. Reservations can be made after April 17 by
calling the park at ☎ 677-2423.

Herb Garden: A colonial herb garden is maintained by the Friends
of Colonial Pemaquid near the Fort House.

Moorings: Moorings may be obtained through the Bristol Harbor-
master. Contact the town office: ☎ 563-5270 for more information.
Moorings are not maintained for transient use.

Museums: Two museum areas are operated at Colonial Pemaquid. In the main museum, guide books take visitors on a self-guided tour of artifacts that were recovered during archeological excavations, including ceramics, munitions, Native American trade goods, tools, and coins. This museum also contains a diorama of the site as it may have existed during colonial days, and the exhibit entitled "Artifacts in Art," which demonstrates how recovered artifacts may have been used in their day. Exhibits in the tower of Fort William Henry include artifacts from archeological excavations, documents from Forts William Henry and Frederick, and an exhibit of early maps entitled *Norumbega*. One admission fee paid at either museum is good for both areas. Only the main museum is accessible by visitors with mobility challenges.

National Historic Landmark: Colonial Pemaquid State Historic Site was designated as a National Historic Landmark by the US Department of Interior in 1994.

Picnicking: Picnic tables are available on park grounds and on the pier. At present, no charcoal grills are available.

Pier: A pier system with gangway and floats is available for public use. Visitors may arrive by boat and may dock for up to one hour. Renters of permanent moorings may tie up tenders at the floats. The pier is also available for fishing, picnicking, and sightseeing.

Restaurant: The Chart House Restaurant is under new management (1994), and is open daily from 11 am to 9:30 pm, serving traditional American foods and locally harvested seafood, including lobster dinners. Cocktails are available at the inside dining areas. The restaurant season is July 1 - Columbus Day.

Shore Access: Colonial Pemaquid provides shore access to Pemaquid Harbor, at the mouth of the Pemaquid River on Johns Bay.

Toilets: Flush toilet facilities are available at the main museum. These toilets are accessible for the physically challenged.

Tours: Daily tours at 1:30 pm. Tours include grounds and museums. Daily admission fee. Tours last 60 to 90 minutes.

For further information contact: Colonial Pemaquid State Historic Site, PO Box 117, New Harbor, ME 04554. ☎ (207) 677-2423.

Crescent Beach State Park

Location: 8 miles from Portland on ME Route 77 in Cape Elizabeth.

In the 1800's the Ocean House was a popular hotel at Kettle Cove. This was destroyed by fire in 1892. Once a stagecoach line operated between Portland and Bowery Beach (now called Crescent Beach). The Bowery House, also located in this area, was a tavern, later a school, and then a residence. It burned in 1909.

Lobster fishing in the surrounding waters has been a profitable business since the Indians taught the settlers that lobster was edible. In 1830, the first lobster trap appeared in Casco Bay.

Today, Crescent Beach and Kettle Cove provide seashore recreation for the residents of Greater Portland and many vacationers. Kettle Cove is used by local lobstermen and pleasure crafts, but there is no boat launching facility in the area.

Activities: Swimming, fishing, and picnicking.
Facilities: Snack bar, beach, bathhouse with cold water showers, picnic sites with tables and grills, and a children's playground.
Features: Wild animals such as white tail deer, raccoons, skunks, woodchucks, and rabbits inhabit the park. Many songbirds and waterfowl can be viewed.

For further information contact: Crescent Beach State Park, c/o Two Lights State Park, Two Lights Rd., Cape Elizabeth, ME 04107. ☎ (207) 767-3625.

Damariscotta Lake State Park

Location: Off ME Route 32 in Jefferson.

Facilities: Picnic area with tables and grills, shelters on beach.
Activities: Swimming and fishing.

For further information contact: Damariscotta Lake State Park, PO Box 964, Jefferson, ME 04348. ☎ (207) 549-7600.

Eagle Island State Historic Site

Location: Located 3 miles off the coast of Harpswell.

$\mathcal{E}$agle Island was the summer home of North Pole explorer, Admiral Robert E. Peary.

Facilities: Picnic area and pier.

Contact the Maine Bureau of Parks and Recreation for information concerning boats for hire providing transportation to the island. For further information contact: Eagle Island State Historic Site, c/o Dept. of Conservation, RR 1, Box 101, Naples, ME 04055. ☎ (207) 693-6231.

Ferry Beach State Park

Location: On ME Route 9, off Bayview Rd., between Old Orchard Beach and Camp Ellis in Saco.

$\mathcal{A}$ stand of tupelo trees, rare at this latitude, can be seen. This area offers a sweeping view of miles of white sand beaches between the Saco River and Pine Point.

Facilities: Picnic area, changing room, nature trails.
Activities: Swimming, hiking.

For further information contact: Ferry Beach State Park, Bayview Rd., Box 95, Saco, ME 04072. ☎ (207) 283-0067.

Fort Edgecomb State Historic Site

Location: Off US Route 1 south to the Edgecomb end of the Wiscasset Bridge, then next right.

$\mathcal{F}$ort Edgecomb was constructed to protect the picturesque Wiscasset, once the center of the shipping industry north of Boston. This octagonal 1808 blockhouse and earthworks overlook the Sheepscot River, where harbor seals are often seen.

Facilities/Activities: Historic buildings, picnic area, fishing.

For further information contact: Fort Edgecomb State Historic Site, RR 1, Box 89, N. Edgecomb, ME 04556. ☎ (207) 882-7777.

Fort Halifax State Historic Site

Location: 1 mile south of Winslow-Waterville Bridge on US 201.

*B*uilt in 1754, Fort Halifax was the oldest blockhouse in the United States before it was destroyed during the April flood of 1987. A reconstructed blockhouse, which incorporates many artifacts from the 1754 blockhouse, stands on the fort's original site at the confluence of the Kennebec and Sebasticook Rivers in Winslow. Fort Halifax was built at this strategic location in order to protect English colonial settlements along the Kennebec and was garrisoned from 1754-1766.

For further information contact: Fort Halifax State Historic Site, c/o Western Region Headquarters, Center Hill, RR 1, Box 610, Weld, ME 04285. ☎ (207) 585-2661. Fax: (207) 585-2261.

Fort Kent State Historic Site

Location: Off US 1 in the town of Fort Kent.

*T*he Fort Kent blockhouse was constructed in 1839 during the international boundary dispute with Great Britain. It was named for Maine's Governor Edward Kent. This site was part of an extensive fortification and contains a small museum of lumbering and Indian artifacts. In 1891 the Maine legislature authorized $300 for the purchase of the blockhouse, making it Maine's first state-owned historic fort. Today, it is one of Maine's few National Historic Landmarks. The Allagash Wilderness Waterway is a short distance to the west. Clair, New Brunswick lies just across the river from Fort Kent and both the St. Lawrence Seaway and Quebec are within a day's ride.

For further information contact: Fort Kent State Historic Site, c/o Dept. of Conservation, 1235 Central Dr., Presque Isle, ME 04769. ☎ (207) 764-2040 or (207) 834-3866.

Fort Knox State Historic Site

Location: On Route 174, just off US 1, west of the Waldo-Hancock Bridge.

Granite spiral staircases, underground passageways, and three original cannons help one to imagine military life during the Civil War era.

Fort Knox, a splendid example of granite craftsmanship, was constructed from 1844-1869. The narrows of the Penobscot River provide a strategic site for this fortification, which was manned during the Civil and Spanish-American Wars.

The fort was named after Major General Henry Knox, America's first Secretary of War and General George Washington's Commander of Artillery in the American Revolution. General Knox lived in Thomaston, Maine during the final years of his life and was buried there in 1806. America's other Fort Knox, which is located in Kentucky, was also named after him.

Fort Knox's granite was quarried on Mount Waldo, located about five miles upriver from the fort in Frankfort, Maine. The granite blocks were quarried, transported down the mountain, then carried by river barge to Fort Knox's wharf.

Nearly a million dollars was spent in building Fort Knox. Because this money was slow in coming, construction continued for 25 years. When work finally stopped in 1869, the fort was still not completed.

Fort Knox has inspired many legends. One of the better known stories concerns the famous "war willow." During the War of 1812, a farmer rushed on horseback from his farm to warn British warships on the Penobscot River. He grabbed a willow branch, which had been broken from a tree hit by British gunfire, and used the branch as a whip to urge on his horse. After warning his neighbors, who fired at the ships, the farmer returned to his farm and placed the willow branch in the ground. The branch grew into a tree. When the farmer later sold his land to the United States government as the future site of Fort Knox, the tree had reportedly grown to 30 feet high and was as big around as a flour barrel. Local residents supposedly saw the tree in later photographs of the fort, but no photographs or evidence of the famous "war willow" have been found.

The US Department of the Interior named Fort Knox a National Historic Landmark, because it represents a remarkable engineering feat and a stunning example of military architecture.

Facilities: Picnic area. Interpretive guided tours are offered at 1 pm daily (also 11 am on weekends).

For further information contact: Fort Knox State Historic Site, RFD 1, Box 1316, Stockton Springs, ME 04981. ☎ (207) 469-7719.

Fort McClary State Historic Site

Location: From Turnpike and US 1 at rotary in Kittery, travel south 2½ miles on Kittery Point Rd (Rt 103).

Fort McClary is an 1846 blockhouse on the site of fortifications of 1715, 1776, and 1808. Initial use of the site in the early 18th century was to protect Massachusetts vessels from taxation by the New Hampshire colony. Later, use was made of the site during the Revolution, the War of 1812, the Civil War, and the Spanish-American War.

Facilities: Picnic area.

For further information contact: Fort McClary State Historic Site, 28 Old Field Rd., So. Brunswick, ME 03908. ☎ (207) 439-2845.

Fort O'Brien (Fort Machias) State Historic Site

Location: 5 miles from Machias on Route 92.

Fort O'Brien was built in 1775 and rebuilt again in 1777 – destroyed both times by the British. Well-preserved earthworks which overlook Machias Bay were erected for a battery of guns in 1863. The first naval engagement of the Revolution was fought offshore in 1775, five days before the battle at Bunker Hill.

Facilities: Picnic area.

For further information contact: Fort O'Brien (Fort Machias) State Historic Site, c/o Dept. of Conservation, 1235 Central Dr., Presque Isle, ME 04769. ☎ (207) 764-2040.

Fort Point (Fort Pownall) State Park

Location: Off US 1 in Stockton Springs, on the tip of a peninsula jutting into the scenic Pernobscot Bay.

Adjacent to historic Fort Pownall Memorial. Fort Pownall was built in 1759 by Massachusetts Royal Governor Thomas Pownall. To prevent its being taken intact by American patriots, the British burned the wooden fort in 1775 and again in 1779. Only earthworks remain.

Facilities: Scenic road, picnic area, a 200-ft pier for boaters.

For further information contact: Fort Point (Fort Pownall) State Park, c/o Bureau of Parks and Recreation, RR 1, Box 1070, Thomaston, ME 04861. ☎ (207) 596-2253.

Fort Popham State Historic Site

Location: Located 15 miles from Bath on ME Route 209, 2 miles from Popham Beach State Park.

A semi-circular granite fort built in 1861 for use during the Civil War. Modifications were made and the fort was used again in the Spanish-American War and World War I. Historical records conclude that fortifications, probably wooden, existed here and protected the Kennebec settlements during the Revolutionary War and the War of 1812. It was nearby that the English made their first attempt to colonize New England in 1607.

Facilities: Picnic area.
Activities: Fishing.

For further information contact: Fort Popham State Historic Site, c/o Popham Beach State Park, Phippsburg, ME 04562. ☎ (207) 389-1335.

Grafton Notch State Park

Location: Borders ME Route 26 between Upton and Newry.

Several hiking trails dot this scenic area at the end of the Mahoosuc Range. The 2,000-mile Appalachian Trail passes through the park on the way to the northern terminus, Mount Katahdin. Sights include: Screw Auger Falls, Spruce Meadow, Mother Walker Falls, Old Speck Mountain, and Moose Cave. Interpretive panels describe the natural history of the area.

Facilities: Scenic road, picnic area.
Activities: Fishing, hiking.

For further information contact: Grafton Notch State Park, Star Route, Box 330, Newry, ME 04261. ☎ (207) 824-2912.

Holbrook Island Sanctuary

Location: Borders Penobscot Bay south of Bucksport in Brooksville.

Beaches, mud flats, rocky coast, and steep hills that are actually old volcanoes provide for a great diversity of plant and animal life. Observant and alert visitors may see abundant signs of deer, fox, muskrat, beaver, otter, porcupine, bobcat, and coyote. There are also excellent birdwatching opportunities, where one may see great blue herons, ospreys, bald eagles, or peregrine falcons flying.

Facilities: Includes several picnic areas, toilet facilities on both mainland and island (handicap accessible), trails, swimming, launch sites for canoes and kayaks, watchable wildlife sites, possible overnight facilities for study, individual and group sites, a good reference library, and cross-country skiing over the sanctuary. A network of old roads, paths, and animal trails leads visitors to explore the shoreline, marshes, ponds, and forests. In these ecosystems there are rare opportunities to experience an environment controlled by natural forces rather than by human hands.
Activities: Hiking, nature study, cross-country skiing, nature walks (July and August), bird-watching (park provides a bird list), assistance for educational activities on and off the park on nature-related subjects.

For further information contact: Holbrook Island Sanctuary, Box 280, Brooksville, ME 04617. ☎ (207) 326-4012.

John Paul Jones Memorial State Historic Site

Location: On US 1 in the center of Kittery.

John Paul Jones Memorial State Historic Site commemorates the nearby area where, in 1777, the USS Ranger was built and launched. On this ship, Jones received the first salute from a foreign power given to a man-of-war flying the Stars and Stripes.

For further information contact: John Paul Jones Memorial State Historic Site, c/o Dept. of Conservation, RR 1, Box 101, Naples, ME 04055. ☎ (207) 693-6231.

Katahdin Iron Works State Historic Site

Location: From ME 11, drive 5 miles north of Brownville Junction, then take the gravel road 6 miles to "K.I.W."

This Historic Site was once a thriving iron works built in 1843. A restored blast furnace and charcoal kiln remind visitors of an effort that produced nearly 2,000 tons of raw iron annually for half a century. Charcoal was made in 16 kilns consuming 10,000 cords of wood a year.

Facilities: Picnic area (not designated).

For further information contact: Katahdin Iron Works State Historic Site, c/o Western Region Headquarters, Center Hill, RR 1, Box 610, Weld, ME 04285. ☎ (207) 585-2261. Fax (207) 585-2261.

Lake St. George State Park

Location: Adjacent to ME Route 3 in Liberty.

Facilities: Campsites, picnic area, beach, bathhouse, showers, boat launch.

Activities: Camping, swimming, boating, fishing, snowmobiling, hiking, cross-country skiing.

For further information contact: Lake St. George State Park, Liberty, ME 04949. ☎ (207) 589-4255.

Lamoine State Park

Location: On ME 184, 8 miles from Ellsworth near Acadia National Park.

Facilities: Includes campsites, picnic area, and boat launch.
Activities: Camping, boating, fishing.

For further information contact: Lamoine State Park, Route 2, Box 194, Ellsworth, ME 04605. ☎ (207) 667-4778.

Lily Bay State Park

Location: 8 miles north of Greenville on east shore of 40-mile Moosehead Lake.

Facilities: Campsites, picnic area, two boat launch sites, and a beach.
Activities: Camping, swimming, boating, fishing, snowmobiling, hiking, cross-country skiing.

For further information contact: Lily Bay State Park, HC 76, Box 425, Greenville, ME 04441. ☎ (207) 695-2700.

Montpelier State Historic Site

Location: On US 1, one mile east of Thomaston.

Montpelier is a handsome replica of the original mansion built in 1793 and contains most of the original possessions of Major General Knox. At age 31 Knox became the youngest major general of the time, a great war hero, and is credited with planning the battles won by General Washington. After the Revolution, he served for 10 years as the first Secretary of War.

For further information contact: Montpelier State Historic Site, PO Box 83, Thomaston, ME 04861. ☎ (207) 354-8062.

Moose Point State Park

Location: On US 1 between Belfast and Searsport,
overlooking Penobscot Bay.

Facilities: Picnic area.

For further information contact: Moose Point State Park, 310 West Main St., Searsport, ME 04974. ☎ (207) 548-2882.

Mt. Blue State Park

Location: 14 miles from Wilton, off ME Route 156 in Weld,
or 14 miles from Dixfield off Route 142.

$\mathcal{L}$ake Webb provides excellent fishing for small-mouth bass, white perch, pickerel, brown trout, brook trout, and salmon. Brook trout can also be found in many of the region's streams. Mt. Blue's main hiking trail begins three and a half miles beyond the Center Hill Picnic Area. The trail is one and a half miles long and leads to an old fire tower at Mt. Blue's 3,18-foot summit. Other mountains in the region such as Tumbledown and Little Jackson also have good hiking trails.

Park Season And Hours: May 15 through Oct. 1, open daily 9 am to sunset.
Size: 5021.8 acres.
Facilities: Campsites, picnic area, beach, bathhouse, boat launch, amphitheater, recreation hall, Adirondack shelters (available for large group use), canoe rental. A hard surfaced public boat launching ramp is available. Boats and canoes may also be rented from the park ranger. A Recreation Hall, located near the park's amphitheater and water front, includes a large fireplace and provides a sheltered area for nature study activities.
Activities: Camping, swimming, boating canoeing, fishing, snowmobiling, hiking, cross-country skiing, interpretive program. Evening programs. Guided nature walks along the shoreline are also

available at Mt. Blue State Park. Check the bulletin board at the control station for schedules.

For further information contact: Mount Blue State Park, Center Hill, RR 1, Box 610, Weld, ME 04285. ☎ (207) 585-2347. Fax (207) 585-2261.

Peacock Beach State Park

Location: Off ME Route 201 on Pleasant Pond in Richmond, about 10 miles from Augusta.

Facilities: Beach, picnic area.
Activities: Swimming, picnicking.

For further information contact: Peacock Beach State Park, RFD 1, Box 2288, Gardiner, ME 04345. ☎ (207) 582-2813.

Peaks-Kenny State Park

Location: Located in the mountains on the shore of Sebec Lake, at the end of ME Route 153, about 6 miles from Dover-Foxcroft.

Size : 800 acres.
Facilities: Include numerous campsites, showers, beach, bathhouse, picnic area.
Activities: Camping, swimming, fishing, hiking, amphitheater program, roller skating nearby.

For further information contact: Peaks-Kenny State Park, RFD 1, Box 48K, Dover-Foxcroft, ME 04426. ☎ (207) 564-2003.

Popham Beach State Park

Location: Take ME Route 209, 14 miles from Bath to Phippsburg.

Facilities: Picnic area, beach, bathhouse, showers.
Activities: Swimming, fishing.

For further information contact: Popham Beach State Park, Phippsburg, ME 04562. ☎ (207) 389-1335.

Quoddy Head State Park

Location: 4 miles off ME Route 189 at Lubec.

The easternmost point of land in the United States marked by a lighthouse is adjacent to the park. Scenic trails includes rock cliffs rising from the ocean 80 feet below, dense evergreen forest, and a fragile peat bog with unique flowers.

Facilities: Picnic area.
Activities: Hiking, whale and bird watching.

For further information contact: Quoddy Head State Park, RR 2, Box 1490, Lubec, ME 04652. ☎ (207) 764-2040, November 1 thru March 31. ☎ (207) 733-0911, April 1 thru October 31.

Range Ponds State Park

Location: Just off Empire Rd. in Poland. Empire Rd. is approached from ME Route 122; take Route 26 north from Gray, or Route 202 south from Lewiston to connect with ME 122.

Facilities: Day-use park with picnic area, ballfield, boat launch to accommodate those visitors interested in swimming, boating, fishing, cross-country skiing.

For further information contact: Range Ponds State Park, PO Box 475, Poland Spring, ME 04274. ☎ (207) 998-4104.

Rangeley Lake State Park

Location: Reached from Rumford via ME 17 or from Farmington via ME 4.

Campers, swimmers, and fishermen will enjoy the campsites, picnic area, showers, boat launch site, children's play area. Hiking trails; dumping station, pay phone, and firewood also available.

Photographers will find some of the most beautiful scenery in the state in this region of mountains and lakes.

The Rangeley region is famous for landlocked salmon and trout fishing. Anglers who voluntarily "catch and release" contribute to quality fishing.

Wildlife in the area include deer and the majestic moose, as well as many different types of birds and water fowl.

For further information contact: Rangeley Lake State Park, HC 32, Box 5000, Rangeley, ME 04970. ☎ (207) 864-3858.

Reid State Park

Location: 14 miles from Woolwich on ME Route 127.

Nearly a mile and a half of sand beaches, dunes, marshes, ledges, and ocean, plus a warm saltwater pond for swimming, make Reid one of Maine's most popular saltwater parks.

Size: 770 acres.
Facilities: Includes a snack bar, bathhouse, and picnic area.

For further information contact: Reid State Park, Georgetown, ME 04548. ☎ (207) 371-2303.

Roque Bluffs State Park

Location: Located 6 miles off US 1 in Roque Bluffs.

A variety of plant life, such as swamp and pasture roses, and trees such as red maple, birch, spruce, and alder, abound here. The freshwater pond is home to brown and brook trout and beavers. Bobcats and black bears are also inhabitants of the area. Observers may be able to spot ospreys and bald eagles.

Size: 275 acres.
Facilities: Picnic area, changing rooms, pebble beach, and freshwater pond.

For further information contact: Roque Bluffs State Park, RFD, Box 202, Machias, ME 0464. ☎ (207) 255-3475.

Sebago Lake State Park

Location: Off US 302 between Naples and South Casco.

The clear water of Sebago Lake provides Portland's water supply and supports a high quality freshwater sport fishery for salmon and togue. Songo Lock is nearby and permits a boat trip up the Songo River to Long Lake.

Facilities: Numerous campsites, snack bar, picnic area, beaches, bathhouses, boat launch, amphitheater, nature trails.

For further information contact: Sebago Lake State Park, RR 1, Box 101, Naples, ME 04055. ☎ (207) 693-6613, between June 20 and Labor Day. ☎ (207) 693-6231, before June 20 and after Labor Day.

Songo Lock State Historic Site

Location: Between Long Lake and Sebago Lake on the Songo River in Naples.

Songo Lock was first constructed in 1830. Built of stone masonry with wooden gates, the original lock was 90 feet long and 26 feet wide. The Sebago Improvement Company increased the length of the lock to 110 feet and the width to 28 feet when they rebuilt it in 1911. The lock, which is adjacent to Sebago Lake State Park, provides passage between Sebago Lake and Long Lake for recreational boaters.

For further information contact: Songo Lock State Historic Site, c/o Dept. of Conservation, RR 1, Box 101, Naples, ME 04055. ☎ (207) 693-6231.

Swan Lake State Park

Location: North of Swanville off ME Route 141.

Size: 66 acres.
Facilities: Picnic area and several trails.
Activities: Swimming, fishing, hiking.

For further information contact: Swan Lake State Park, Swanville, ME 04841. ☎ (207) 525-4404.

Two Lights State Park

Location: Off ME 77 in Cape Elizabeth.

Dedicated in 1961, Two Lights State Park encompasses 41 acres of rocky headland and associated uplands. From here scenic view of Casco Bay and the open Atlantic can be had. The park's name is derived from the two nearby adjacent lighthouses, which operated from 1828 to 1924. The twin lights were the first to be erected on the Maine coast. Originally constructed of rubble stone, the lights were replaced with cast iron structures in 1873.

Today, the eastern light operates automatically with the four million candlepower lamp visible 17 miles at sea. The western lighthouse is now inoperative and privately owned. Neither of the two lighthouses are located in the park. They may not be visited but can be seen at the end of Two Lights Road.

During World War II, this area was an army coastal fortification. The bunker, located near the center shoreline of the park, was an underground control center and storage depot. This is closed for the safety of the public. The cement tower on north ridge was used for observation, range finding, and triangular plotting. The tower is not open to the public at this time.

The unusual Cape Elizabeth rock formation has resulted from the action of the surf on alternating layers of hard and soft material. The result of this weathering action is rock with a surface texture and color similar to petrified wood.

Facilities: Picnic sites, a small playground, two group sites and a shelter for group activities are reservable. Crescent Beach State Park is only a half-mile away.

Trails: Numerous footpaths provide opportunities to enjoy the spectacular ocean view as well as the beautiful wildflowers and birds.

For further information contact: Two Lights State Park, Two Lights Rd., Cape Elizabeth, ME 04107. ☎ (207) 799-5871.

Vaughan Woods State Park

Location: South on Route 236 out of Berwick, on banks of Salmon Falls River.

Facilities: Picnic area and nature trails to accommodate hikers and cross-country skiers.

Special Interest: In 1634, here at "Cow Cove" the first cows in this part of the country were landed from the ship *The Pied Cow.*

For further information contact: Vaughan Woods State Park, c/o Dept. of Conservation, RR 1, Box 101, Naples, ME 04055. ☎ (207) 693-6231.

Warren Island State Park

Location: A 70-acre, spruce-covered island in Penobscot Bay.

Facilities: Includes campsites, two Adirondack shelters, fresh drinking water, picnic area, docking and mooring facilities. Contact Camden Hill State Park for information about campsite availability on a day-to-day basis.

The park is designed for the boating public, so there is no public ferry to the island.

For further information contact: Warren Island State Park, c/o Bureau of Parks and Recreation, RR 1, Box 1070, Thomaston, ME 04861. ☎ (207) 236-3109.

Wolfe's Neck Woods State Park

Location: On Wolfe's Neck Rd., south of US 1 in Freeport.

Size: 243 acres.
Facilities: Picnic area.
Hiking: Self-guided trails and guided nature walks along the Casco Bay and Harraseeket River are the most popular activities.

For further information contact: Wolfe's Neck Woods State Park, Wolfe's Neck Rd., Freeport, ME 04032. ☎ (207) 865-4465.

National Parks

Acadia National Park

Location: Mount Desert Island is reached by automobile on ME Route 3. Schoodic Peninsula is reached by ME Route 186.

Early History

$\mathcal{D}$eep shell heaps indicate the presence of Indian encampments dating back 6,000 years in Acadia National Park, but prehistoric records are scanty. The first written descriptions of Maine coast Indians, recorded 100 years after European trade contacts began, describe native Americans who lived off the land by hunting, fishing, collecting shellfish, and gathering plants and berries. The Abnaki Indians knew Mount Desert Island as Pemetic, "the sloping land." They built bark-covered, conical shelters, and traveled in exquisitely designed birchbark canoes. Historical notes record that the Abnaki wintered in interior forests and spent their summers near the coast. Archaeological evidence suggests the opposite pattern. In order to avoid harsh inland winters and to take advantage of salmon runs upstream, Indians wintered on the coast and summered inland.

The first meeting between the people of Pemetic and the Europeans is a matter of conjecture. But it was a Frenchman, Samuel Champlain, who made the first important contribution to the historical record of Mt. Desert Island. He led the expedition that landed on Mt. Desert on September 5, 1604 and wrote in his journal, "the mountain summits are all bare and rocky.... I name it Isles des Monts Desert." Champlain's visit to Acadia, 16 years before the Pilgrims landed at Plymouth Rock, destined this land to become known as New France before it became New England.

In 1613, French Jesuits, welcomed by Indians, established the first French mission in America on what is now Fernald Point, near the entrance to Somes Sound. They had just begun to build a fort, plant their corn, and baptize the natives when an English ship, commanded by Captain Samuel Argall, destroyed their mission.

The English victory at Fernald Point doomed Jesuit claims on Mount Desert Island. The land was in a state of limbo, lying between the French to the north, and the British, whose settlements were in Massachusetts and southward. No one wished to settle in this contested territory. For the next 150 years, Mt. Desert Island's importance was primarily its use as a landmark for seamen.

There was a brief period when it seemed Mount Desert would again become a center of French activity. In 1688, Antoine Laumet, an ambitious young man who had immigrated to New France and bestowed upon himself the title Sieur de la Mothe Cadillac, asked for and received a hundred thousand acres of land along the Maine coast, including all of Mt. Desert. Cadillac's hopes of establishing a feudal estate in the New World, however, were short lived. Although he and his bride resided there for a time, they soon abandoned their enterprise. Cadillac later gained lasting recognition as the founder of Detroit.

In 1759, after a century and a half of conflict, British troops triumphed at Quebec, ending French dominion in Acadia. With Indians scattered and the fleur-de-lis banished, lands along the Maine coast opened for English settlement. Governor Francis Bernard of Massachusetts obtained a royal land grant on Mt. Desert Island. In 1760, Bernard attempted to secure his claim by offering free land to settlers. Abraham Somes and James Richardson accepted the offer and settled their families at what is now Somesville.

The onset of the Revolutionary War ended Bernard's plans for Mount Desert Island. In its aftermath, Bernard lost his claim, and the newly created United States of America granted the western half of Mount Desert Island to John Bernard, son of the governor, and the eastern half of the island to Marie Therese de Gregopire, grandaughter of Cadillac. Bernard and de Gregoire soon sold their landholdings to non-resident landlords.

Their real estate transactions probably made very little difference to the increasing number of settlers homesteading on Mount Desert Island. By 1820, farming and lumbering vied with fishing and shipbuilding as major occupations. Settlers converted hundreds of acres of trees into wood products ranging from schooners and barns to baby cribs and hand tools. Farmers harvested wheat, rye, corn and potatoes. By 1850, the familiar sights of fishermen and sailors, fish racks and shipyards, revealed a way of life linked to the sea.

It was the outsiders – artists and journalists – who revealed and popularized this island to the world in the mid-1800's. Painters of the Hudson River School, including Thomas Cole and Frederic Church, glorified Mount Desert Island with their brushstrokes, inspiring patrons and friends to flock here. These were the rusticators. Undaunted by crude accommodations and simple food, they sought out local fishermen and farmers to put them up for a modest fee. Summer after summer, the rusticators returned to renew friendships with local islanders and, most of all, to savor the fresh salt air, beautiful scenery, and relaxed pace. Soon the villagers' cottages and fishermen's huts filled to overflowing, and by 1880 30 hotels competed for vacationers' dollars. Tourism was becoming a major industry.

For a select handful of Americans, the 1880's and the "gay nineties" meant affluence on an unprecedented scale. Mount Desert, still remote from the cities of the East, became a retreat for prominent people of the times. The Rockefellers, Morgans, Fords, Vanderbilts, Carnegies, and Astors, chose to spend their summers here. Not content with the simple lodgings then available, these families transformed the landscape of Mount Desert Island with elegant estates, euphemistically called cottages. Luxury, refinement, and ostentatious gatherings replaced buckboard rides, picnics, and day-long hikes of an earlier era. For over 40 years, the wealthy held sway at Mount Desert, but the Great Depression and World War II marked the end of such extravagance. The final blow came in 1947 when a fire of monumental proportions consumed many of the great estates.

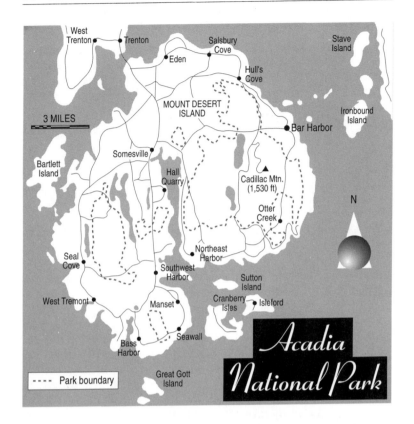

Though the affluent of the turn of the century came here to frolic, they had much to do with preserving the landscape that we know today. It was from this social stratum that George B. Dorr, a tireless spokesman for conservation, devoted 43 years of his life, energy, and family fortune to preserving the Acadian landscape. In 1901 he was disturbed by the growing development of the Bar Harbor area and the dangers he foresaw in the newly invented gasoline powered portable sawmill. George Dorr and others established the Hancock County Trustees of Public Reservations. The corporation, whose sole purpose was to preserve land for the perpetual use of the public, acquired 6000 acres by 1913. Dorr offered the land to the federal government, and in 1916, President Wilson announced the creation of Sieur de Monts National Monument. Dorr continued to acquire property and renewed his efforts to obtain full national park status for his beloved preserve. In 1919 President Wilson signed the act establishing Lafayette National Park, the first national park east of the Mississippi. Dorr, whose labors constituted "the greatest of one-man shows in the history of land conservation" became the first park superintendent.

In 1929, the park name changed to Acadia. Today the park encompasses 35,000 acres, and the simple pleasures of "ocean, forests, lakes and mountains" that for over a century and a quarter have been sought and found by millions, are yours to enjoy.

If you have never tried – really tried – doing nothing, Acadia is a good place to begin. You need a rocky ledge or stony beach, perhaps at Schoodic Point, along Ocean Drive, or near Seawall. Sit down and relax and wait for things to happen. A gull may sail up over the ledge with a sea urchin in its beak. The gull drops the urchin onto the rocks below to smash its shell-like, spiny armor. The gull dives right behind the creature and then devours it. Besides watching the activity, listen for the chuckle of pebbles moving in the surf and smell the salt air as the sun warms your skin. Doing nothing on the shore is an art, a pleasure, and a long-standing tradition.

Little of New England's rockbound coast remains in public ownership. Undeveloped and natural, Acadia National Park preserves the beauty of part of Maine's coast, its coastal mountains, and its offshore islands. Weather permitting, you can drive to the top of Cadillac Mountain, the highest point, for a spectacular view of this coast. Or better yet, park your car and walk or bike into the nature and history of the park on its many trails.

Acadia, as the name suggests, was French before it was English, then American. French frigates hid from English men-of-war in Frenchman Bay, screened from detection by the Porcupine Islands. The French and English battled for possession of North America from 1613 until 1760. French explorer Samuel de Champlain sailed into the Bay in 1604 and named this Mount Desert Island because of its landmark bare top.

The sea encircles, thrusts inland, and fogs here. In the midday sun its bright-blue surface is studded with lobster buoys. In fog all is gray and muted. Somewhere out at sea engines may mutter, but the lobster boat is blurred or lost in a formless world. Seen at sundown from Cadillac Mountain, the sea glows in soft pinks, mauve, and gold. Gulls wing silently home to distant islands, and, like fireflies, navigational aids flash warnings from reefs, islands, and headland.

Between the sea and the forested mountains is the small, fascinating world of the tidal zone. Twice daily exposed to air and drowned by sea water, it is a world of specially adapted organisms. Tidepools, pockets of seawater stranded in rock basins, are microhabitats brimming with life and exposed to view. In these natural aquariums you can watch marine animals going about their business. This zone of life is amplified by Acadia's tides, which vary from nine to 14 feet, averaging 11 to 12 feet. It is the primeval meeting place of earth and water.

Behind the sea lie Acadia's forests and mountains, made easy for exploring by an extensive system of carriage roads. These broad, smooth, graveled byways encircle Jordan Pond and Eagle Lake and wind around the flanks of Sargent and Penobscot Mountains. They offer stunning views of Somes Sound and Frenchman Bay. They lead you along beaver-dammed brooks. The grades are gentle, but the vistas are long. A bicycle path loops around Eagle Lake.

The story of the people who lived on this island when Champlain first saw it is told with Indian artifacts and exhibits in the Abbe Museum at Sieur de Monts Spring. Take the ferry to Little Cranberry Island to see the Islesford Museum, whose ship models, tools, and pictures reveal island life in the 19th and early 20th centuries.

Villages near the park present the variety of lifestyles on the island today. Northeast Harbor shelters sailboats, large and small, and a summer colony. Bar Harbor caters to tourists, offering many accommodations and amusements. Bass Harbor and Southwest Harbor, and Winter Harbor at Schoodic, retain more of the traditional flavor of Maine coastal villages. Those who earn livings from the sea – whether lobstering, fishing, building boats, or guarding the coast – tie up here. And canneries, lobster pounds, and boatyards have not yet been replaced by summer homes and motels.

You may wonder who built the carriage roads and who envisioned a national park in this tourist area. This national park is unusual because it was neither carved out of public lands nor bought with public funds. It was envisioned and donated through the efforts of private citizens. Many people loved Mount Desert Island, Schoodic Peninsula, and the nearby islands. Maine residents and summer visitors alike donated their time and resources to preserve Acadia's beauty. George B. Dorr and Charles W. Eliot, a former president of Harvard University, saw the dangers of development and acted to avoid them. John D. Rockefeller, Jr., also played a critical role. He built the carriage roads and gave more than 11,000 acres, about one-third of the park's area, to what became known as Acadia National Park.

Trails & Paths

The more than 120 miles of trails in the park range from short, level surf walks, to the steep Precipice Trail. Connecting trails enable hardy hikers to scale several Acadia peaks in one trip. Between 1915 and 1933, John D. Rockefeller, Jr. financed and directed the building of 57 miles of carriage roads; a network of woodland roads free of motor vehicles for hikers, bicyclists, horseback riders, and carriages. Activities on some of the 50 miles of carriage roads of the park include cross-country skiing and snowmobiling. The Eagle Lake Loop Road is specially graded for bicycles.

Lighthouses

The French explorer Champlain, who named Mount Desert Island and Isle au Haut, ran aground here in 1604. His was the first of many boating mishaps on these shores. The rocky shoreline, hidden ledges, and fog posed hazards until after the Civil War. By that time foghorns and lights were installed to make navigation generally safe. Today the US Coast Guard maintains five lighthouses in this area: Egg Rock, Bass Harbor Head, Bear Island, Baker Island, and Great Duck Island. The romance of the often lonely life of lightkeepers and their families is a thing of the past. Modernized lighthouses are run by remote control.

History

After its discovery in 1604, Mount Desert Island played a part in French, English, and Indian contact – and conflict. French ships hid in Frenchman Bay during the French and Indian War between France and England. The French would rendezvous with Indians who canoed down the rivers to trade. English colonists settled here after the British victory in Canada in 1760, when the threat of continual warfare ended.

Commercial Fishing

Commercial fishing remains an important industry in Maine. Fishing is no longer the hazardous producer of widows and orphans as in sailing days, but today's practitioners remain salty, colorful characters. Most prized is the lobster, but scallops, crabs, and various fish are caught commercially. At low tide, clam diggers often work the flats with their short rakes. Boat building continues on the island and Schoodic Peninsula.

Glaciers and the Landscape

Mount Desert Island's major valleys all run north and south and each holds one or two lakes that the glaciers scooped out. Erratic boulders sit where the mammoth ice sheet, two miles thick in places, stranded them. Many rocks are polished or scratched by the glaciers. Some Sound, the only fjord on the east coast of the United States, is a glacial river valley drowned by the sea.

Seasons

Be prepared for changeable weather conditions. In the summer, high temperatures are usually 70 to 80° F. Fog is common. Spring and fall are cooler, with highs usually 50 to 60° F. In the winter, which lasts from November to April in Acadia, highs are around 30° F, while nighttime lows may be below zero. Annual snowfall is about 60 inches.

Camping

You may camp at either of two campgrounds: Blackwoods, on Route 3 five miles south of Bar Harbor, or Seawall on Route 102A four miles south of Southwest Harbor. All park campsites are situated in woods, within a 10 minute walk of the ocean. One vehicle, six people, and two small tents or one large tent are allowed at a campsite. Designated campsites accommodate trailers up to 35 feet. Neither campground has utility hook-ups. From late spring to early fall, the campgrounds provide comfort stations, cold running water, dump station, picnic tables, fire rings, water faucets, and amphitheaters for evening programs. Showers and a camping supply store are within a half mile of both campgrounds. Facilities are limited to picnic tables, fire rings, pit toilets, and a hand pump for drinking water. Camping fees are subject to change. Camping fees and entrance fees are separate charges. Blackwoods Campground (reservations required in summer) is open all year. Camping at Seawall (open May-Sept.) is first-come, first-served. There are private campgrounds in neighboring towns.

Facilities and Activities

- Acadia has many foot trails, ranging from lowland paths to rugged mountain routes. Carriage roads are open to bicycles (you may rent them in nearby towns). Some are open to horses and horse-drawn carriages. Carriage tours are available at Wildwood Stables. Bicycles are not allowed on hiking trails.
- Naturalist Programs Schedules are available at the visitor center, park headquarters, and park campgrounds. Available are walks led by naturalists, children's programs, hikes, and boat cruises. There are evening programs at the campgrounds.
- Boat operators offer rentals, charters, cruises, and ferry service in nearby towns. Information available at the visitor center.
- Freshwater fishing requires a state license (available in town offices). No license is required for saltwater fishing.
- Lifeguards are on duty in summer at Echo Lake (freshwater) and Sand Beach (saltwater). The ocean is cold!
- Cross-country skiing, snowmobiling, ice fishing, and winter hiking are popular. Blackwoods Campground is open in winter.

Rules and Regulations

- Pets are allowed but must be on a leash at all times and may not be left unattended.
- All camping must be done in established campgrounds. Overnight backpacking is prohibited because the park is small and fragile. If you wish to camp at one of the 12 nearby private campgrounds, please see section titled *Other Accommodations* for the addresses of local Chambers of Commerce.

For reservations or other information write: Superintendent, Acadia National Park, Bar Harbor, ME 04609. ☎ (207) 288-3338, voice or TDD.

Saint Croix Island

Location: The entrance to St. Croix Island International Historic Site is 8 miles south of Calais, Maine, along US 1. There is currently no ferry to the island.

$\mathcal{I}$n the century after Columbus's first voyage to the Americas, few serious attempts at colonization were made in North America. Even Spain, which completely dominated colonial ventures throughout the 16th century, confined its efforts almost exclusively to the area south of the Rio Grande. By 1600 only about 20,000 Spaniards were living in the Western Hemisphere.

The first attempts at colonization by the French at Fort Caroline in Florida and by the English at Roanoke Island in North Carolina had been half-hearted, poorly financed, and ill-supplied. But as the power of these nations increased and that of Spain declined, they sent out more determined expeditions to the New World.

On November 8, 1603, King Henry IV of France granted a patent to Pierre de Gua, Sieur de Monts, making him a lieutenant general with full authority over all North America between the 40th and 46th parallels (from present-day Philadelphia to beyond Montreal). He was directed to "establish the name, power, and authority of the King of France; to summon the natives to a knowledge of the Christian religion; to people, cultivate, and settle the said lands; to make explorations and especially to seek out mines of precious metals." De Monts gathered his supplies and ships and selected the company during the winter of 1603-1604.

The Company was an odd mixture of men. Some were of noble birth and not used to hard work. Others were carpenters, masons, stonecarvers, and tailors. The records also show that a company of Swiss mercenaries accompanied the expedition. No women were part of this first venture; they were to join the Community later. Perhaps the most valuable member of the party was Samuel de Champlain, whom Henry IV commissioned as geographer. Champlain was a seasoned explorer who had visited the Saint Lawrence Valley the previous year. His report to Henry IV on the Spanish Colonies in South America had earlier won him royal praise. The King encouraged him to found a permanent French colony in North America.

De Monts' first ship sailed from Le Havre on March 7, 1604. The second ship left three days later. After a long, stormy voyage the party reached land at Sable Island, about 160 nautical miles east-southeast of present-day Halifax. Almost colliding with the island, they made it to the mainland and began to explore, working south and west around the coast into the Bay of Fundy, named La Bay Francaise by De Monts. In the last week of June they came to Passamaquoddy Bay and sailed up the St. Croix River. They came upon an island which Champlain described as "covered with firs, birches, maples, and oaks. It is by nature very well situated. Vessels could pass up the river only at the mercy of the cannon on this island, and we deemed the location most advantageous." De Monts named the island Saint Croix because just above it two long coves meet with the river to form a cross.

The men set about constructing fortifications and shelters according to plans drawn up by Champlain. The most strongly built structures were the governor's dwelling and a storehouse. They also built a blacksmith shop, an ovenhouse, a kitchen, barracks for soldiers, and dwellings for the gentlemen and artisans.

Toward the end of August, De Monts decided to send the two large ships back to France, leaving only two small boats of seven and 15 tons with the 79 who stayed. Taking one of these boats, Champlain, with 12 sailors and two Indians, began exploring down the coast of Maine and got as far as Pemaquid Point before lack of provisions and bad weather forced them to turn back.

Winter set in and the colonists found themselves in a wilderness rougher than they had expected. The first snow fell October 6, and by December 3 Champlain recorded that ice had moved down the river past the island. Frozen cider was doled out by the pound. A multitude of factors compounded the loneliness: poor shelter, only salted food, insufficient clothing, complete isolation, and the knowledge that the next ship from France was not due until April. Many became ill with scurvy and, at winter's end, 35 were dead.

As winter gave way to spring a feeling of relief spread in the community. But when April passed and no supply ship had arrived, anxiety began to mount. The ship finally arrived on June 15. Two days later, de Monts set out to find a better site for the settlement. His search ended across the Bay of Fundy at Port Royal, near the present town of Annapolis Royal. Soon the basic framework of the principal dwellings at Saint Croix was moved to Port Royal and the island was abandoned.

Though the French colonists had spent only one winter here, their efforts to colonize North America did not end with the abandonment of Saint Croix. The settlement at Port Royal survived and soon other Frenchman arrived. In July 1608, Champlain founded the village which has grown into Quebec City. Today the language, culture, and religion of royal France, whose rule over the Saint Lawrence Valley lasted until 1763, live on in the Province of Quebec.

During the next few years, people from Port Royal would occasionally visit the island of St. Croix. Historian Marc Lescarbot noted that vegetables were still growing in the abandoned gardens among the ruins. In 1613, Capt. Samuel Argall of Virginia, commissioned to clear all foreign settlements to the 45th parallel, burned the remaining buildings of St. Croix.

After Argall departed, nature regained control of the island. Even the name was forgotten and New England settlers came to know the place as Dochet Island. Only in 1789 when the boundary between the United States and Canada was being determined did the boundary commissioners rediscover the old name. In later years the island served as a neutral meeting place during the War of 1812 for British and American officials, and as a farm. The St. Croix River Light, established in 1857, is still maintained by the Coast Guard as a navigational beacon.

At Port Royal National Historic Park in Nova Scotia, Canada, you can see a reconstruction of the village founded after St. Croix was abandoned.

For further information: St. Croix Island International Historic Site is administered by the National Park Service, US Department of the Interior, in cooperation with the Canadian Government. The superintendent of Acadia National Park, whose address is Route 1, Box 1, Bar Harbor, ME 04609, is in immediate charge.

Massachusetts

State Parks

You can still experience the wilderness in Massachusetts far from the sounds of the city, by exploring the many parks, forests and wildlife management areas in the state. Every citizen of the state lives within 10 miles of a public park, forest, or wildlife area. These sanctuaries are areas of superb recreational, archaeological, or scenic characteristics unique to Massachusetts. The sites have been carefully selected to be large enough to ensure the preservation of nature in the park.

Outdoor recreational opportunities attract tourists as well as residents. Some of the finest fishing waters in North America can be found within Massachusetts' lakes. Fishermen share the lakes with swimmers, boaters, and even water skiers.

State Agencies

For further information on state parks, forests, and refuges areas contact:

Massachusetts Division of Forests and Parks
100 Cambridge St.
Boston, MA 02202
☎ (617) 727-3180

For further information on the wildlife management areas contact:

Division of Fisheries and Wildlife
100 Cambridge St.
Boston, MA 02202
☎ (617) 727-3151

Arcadia Nature Center & Wildlife Sanctuary

Location: From I-91, exit 18 near Hope Valley.

The Sanctuary is on the west side of the Connecticut River. Almost half of the site is woody swamp and marsh. Hiking here not recommended. Wild rice was planted some years ago and continues to grow in abundance. The site is at the meeting point of two bird migration routes. The upper half of the site is forested with mixed hardwoods and conifers planted in the early 1900s. This means some wonderful birdwatching opportunities – complete with an observation tower that overlooks the marsh.

Hiking: Over four miles of trails.
Canoeing: Access to the Oxbow and Connecticut River.

For further information contact: Headquarters, Easthampton, MA 01027. ☎ (413) 584-3009.

Beartown State Forest

Location: From Great Barrington, about 5 miles east on SR 23.

This is fabulous country with challenging hills that are part of the Hoosac Range. Mt. Wilcox, at the Forest center, is 2,150 feet at its highest point and is surrounded by many streams and ponds. The forest is crossed by the Applalachian Trail, so hiking will be memorable.

Birds: Wild turkey, grouse, woodcock, hawks, owls, woodpeckers, finches, crossbills, thrushes, and warblers.
Mammals: Deer, black bear, bobcat, coyote, snowshoe hare, cottontail, red and gray foxes, and porcupine.

Camping: Only 12 sites – very hard to reserve during the late spring and summer months.
Hiking/Backpacking: Five miles of the Appalachian Trail.
Fishing: Trout stocked in streams. Rumor of bass in the ponds.
Swimming: Benedict Pond.
Ski touring: 11 miles of challenging marked trails.

For further information contact: Headquarters, Monterey, MA 01245. ☎ (413) 528-0904.

Birch Hill Wildlife Management Area

Location: Off US 202 at Baldwinville.

The Birch Hill Wildlife Management Area is the largest wildlife management area in central Massachusetts.

The area is crisscrossed with paved and dirt roads that are used more often as hiking and snow trails. Trail bikers appear to use the trails as often as hikers, but indications are that bikes will soon be banned.

Birds: Common species include woodcock, grouse, waterfowl, flycatchers, woodpeckers, warblers, pheasants and turkey.
Mammals: Deer, raccoon, beaver, mink, muskrat, showshoe hare.
Camping: 150 campsites at Lake Dennison, a 32-acre natural lake.
Hiking: More than 30 miles of back roads and trails.
Hunting: Waterfowl and deer.
Fishing: Trout fishing in Miller's River and Priest Brook. Trout stocked.
Canoeing: Both streams within the area can be canoed. Boats with electric motors are allowed only on the lake.

For further information contact: WMA, Birch Hill WMA Headquarters, Area Supervisor, Dennison St., Baldwinville, MA 01436. ☎ (617) 939-8977.

Bolton Flats Wildlife Management Area

Location: From I-495 Exit 27.

The Bolton Flats Wildlife Management Area is wonderful for birding. Most of the area is open agricultural fields and brushfields, with marshy wetlands, maple swamps, and brushy river banks.

Birds: Keep your eyes open for egrets, glossy ibis, herons. In migration, the site is said to "teem" with black duck, mallard, pintail, snow goose, blue goose.
Hunting: Pheasant in season.
Canoeing: Permitted on the Nashua River.

For further information contact: Headquarters, Wildlife District Manager, Temple St., West Boylston, MA 01583. ☎ (508) 835-3607.

Borderland State Park

Location: On Massapoag Avenue in North Easton.

Believe it or not, this was once a country estate. The owners maintained the property as a game and forest preserve, and today it is a delightful state park.

Hiking: On woods roads and trails (hilly on the northside and a little more challenging).

For further information contact: Headquarters, Massapoag Ave., North Easton, MA 02356. ☎ (508) 238-6566.

Brimfield State Forest

Location: Between Sturbridge and Palmer.

Brimfield State Forest is lush with mixed northern hardwoods; the understory includes azalea and laurel. Many wildflowers blossom in season. The forest harbors several fast-flowing streams. Dean Pond is the largest of many small ponds that offer water entertainment. No boats are permitted on Dean Pond.

Hiking: 24 miles of forest roads.
Hunting: Deer, bobcat, rabbit, raccoon, ruffed grouse, woodcock.
Fishing: Abundant trout in streams.

For further information contact: Headquarters, Brimfield, MA
01010. ☎ (413) 245-9966.

Campbell Falls State Park

Location: From New Marlboro on SR 57.

The short trail between the two parking areas passes through
mixed forest with some unusually large white pines and hemlocks.
It crosses what is a modest cascade when the stream is flowing.
There is little to do here except maybe stretch your legs, but there
are seldom any crowds and you get a chance to enjoy the outdoors.

For more information contact: Massachusetts Division of Forests &
Parks,100 Cambridge St., Boston, MA 02202. ☎ (617) 727-3180.

Catamount State Forest

Location: From Shelburne Falls, 1 mile west on SR 2.

Here is a great opportunity for taking a hike in a somewhat lonely
state forest. The scenery consists of interesting terrain: rolling to
hilly, somewhat rugged, with kettleholes, potholes, marsh,
streams, a 47-acre pond, mixed forest.

Hiking: Five miles of foot trails, three miles of woods roads.

For further information contact: Headquarters, c/o Mohawk Trail
State Forest, PO Box 7, Charlemont, MA 01339. ☎ (413) 339-5504.

Chester-Blandford State Forest

Location: Chester, Massachusetts.

Hikers will enjoy this state forest for the challenge. The forested slopes are steep, with many brooks and streams.

Sanderson Brook has a 100-ft. cascade. The road to the falls and brookside trail has been closed to all vehicles, but it's an attractive quarter-mile walk from the parking area.

Camping: 12 sites – usually occupied during the late spring and summer months.
Hiking: Trails and forest roads.
Hunting: Deer, bobcat, snowshoe hare, cottontail, raccoon, woodcock, ruffed grouse.
Fishing: Trout in streams.

For further information contact: Headquarters, Chester, MA 01050. ☎ (413) 354-6347.

Clarksburg State Forest

Location: Northwest corner of the state.

A heavily forested site overlooking the Hoosic River. Trees are mixed hardwoods with white and red pines and spruces. This makes for a wonderful display of fall colors – and the colors do bring in the crowds.

Camping: 47 sites.
Hiking: The Appalachian Trail crosses the Forest.

For further information contact: Headquarters, Middle Road, Clarksburg, MA 01247. ☎ (413) 442-8928.

Crane Pond Wildlife Management Area

Location: From I-95, Exit 54.

$\mathcal{M}$ost of the area is abandoned farmland now reverting to brush and forest. About one-fifth is marsh, bog, and open water. Motor vehicles, including trail bikes and snowmobiles, are not allowed inside. A large network of walking trails are overgrown.

Hunting: Most native game species are present.
Fishing: Trout are stocked in the Parker River.

For further information contact: Headquarters, Wildlife District Manager, Harris St., Box 86, Acton, MA 01720. ☎ (508) 263-4647.

Crane Wildlife Management Area

Location: At the west end of Cape Cod, near Falmouth.

$\mathcal{T}$errain is flat to gently rolling, with a few low ridges. The site has a few small streams and ponds.

A network of trails is often used by hikers and horse riders in spring and summer and on Sundays in hunting season. Common wildlife species include pheasant, quail, woodcock, grouse, deer, fox, rabbit, woodchuck, and squirrel.

For further information contact: Headquarters, Wildlife District Manager, Massachusetts Division of Fisheries and Wildlife, 195 Bournedale Rd., Buzzards Bay, MA 02532. ☎ (508) 759-3406.

D.A.R. State Forest

Location: From Goshen on SR 9, 1mile north on SR 112.

$\mathcal{T}$his is one of the most popular state forests in the state. The biggest attractions include swimming, an attractive campground, an active naturalist program, and pleasant scenery.

Devil's Den is a craggy cleft on Roger's Brook. Upper and Lower Highland lakes are each a bit less than a mile long. One side of Lower Highland has private homes.

About two-thirds of the site is undeveloped except for hiking trails. In this portion are streams, ponds, swamps, and a waterfall.

The Nature Center is where you will find an innovative naturalist program, which includes evening programs, night walks, pond walks, a three-mile nature trail, and special events.

Camping: 58 sites.
Hiking: Nine miles of trails.
Fishing: Bass, perch, trout.
Canoeing: On both lakes.
Swimming: In Upper Lake.

For further information contact: Headquarters, D.A.R. State Forest, Goshen, MA 01032. ☎ (413) 268-7098.

Erving State Forest

Location: From Athol, 8 miles west on SR 2A.

Trees include oak, white pine and hemlock, with mountain laurel, azalea, blueberry, and honeysuckle in the understory. Seasonal wildflowers include painted trillium, Solomon's-seal, bunchberry, clintonia, and mayflower.

Birds: Whip-poor-will, flycatchers, wrens, hawks, owls, grouse, woodcocks, scarlet tanagers, bluebirds, thrushes, warblers, chickadee, titmouse.
Mammals: Raccoon, snowshoe hare, chipmunk, weasel, cottontail, muskrat, beaver, fox, red and gray squirrels, bobcat.
Nature trail: An easy walk of one mile.
Camping: 32 sites.
Hiking: One two-mile trail; 12 miles of forest roads.
Hunting: Deer.
Fishing: Trout in Laurel Lake and streams.

For further information contact: Headquarters, Erving State Forest, Erving, MA 01364. ☎ (413) 544-3939.

Granville State Forest

Location: East of Granville on SR 57.

On the slopes above the river, the forest is largely mature hemlocks with little ground cover. Elsewhere is a fine spring display of mountain laurel. Terrain is steep with many ridges and ravines draining to the Hubbard River.

Camping: Two campgrounds with a total of 40 sites.
Hiking: Three miles of trails in and beyond the Forest.
Hunting: Deer, snowshoe hare, grouse, woodcock.
Fishing: Trout stocked in season.
Swimming: Stream and small pond.
Ski touring/Snowmobiling: 11 miles of unplowed roads.

For further information contact: Headquarters, Granville State Forest, Granville, MA 01034. ☎ (413) 357-6611.

H. O. Cook State Forest

Location: On the Massachusetts/Vermont border.

H.O. Cook State Forest is highlighted by rugged, forested terrain that is sharply dissected by several large streams. Elsewhere the pattern is similiar to other parts of the state: northern hardwoods with red spruce. Azalea and hobblebush are prominent in the understory. Wildflowers abound in open areas of the forest.

Hiking: Six miles of little-used forest roads.

For further information contact: Headquarters, c/o Mohawk Trail State Forest, PO Box 7, Charlemont, MA 01339. ☎ (413) 339-5504.

Harold Parker State Forest

Location: Southeast of Andover.

The original forest was cut or burned several generations ago, followed by farming and pasturing. Now there is a mature forest

cover, some developing through succession and extensive plantations. The site includes 10 ponds and wooded swamps.

Harold Parker State Forest is considered poor for birding, due to
the high number of hikers and campers and nearby traffic.

Camping: 134 sites.
Hiking: Trails and woods roads throughout the site.
Hunting: Limited amounts of pheasant and snowshoe hare. Re-
strictions for hunters.
Fishing: Berry Pond is stocked with trout. Bass in ponds.

For further information contact: Headquarters, Harold Parker State
Forest, Middleton Rd., North Andover, MA 01845. ☎ (508) 686-
3391.

High Ridge Wildlife Management Area

Location: Northcentral Massachusetts near Gardner.

*I*nterestingly, this was once a mental hospital surrounded by farm
fields. The buildings across the railroad tracks are now a minimum
security prison and, obviously, off-limits. Only foot travel is permitted beyond the parking area.

A unique mix of agricultural fields, brushy fields, and hardwood
forest provides the habitats favored by many wildlife species. Two
small streams with native trout supply several marshy areas.

Wildlife: Deer, waterfowl, grouse, woodcock, rabbit.

For further information contact: Headquarters, Wildlife District
Manager, Temple St., West Boylston, MA 01583. ☎ (508) 835-3607.

Hinsdale Flats Wildlife Management Area

Location: East of Pittsfield.

*T*he East Branch of the Housatonic is near the western boundary
of the wildlife management area. Bilodeau Brook bisects the area.
The area has two small artificial ponds and a beaver pond.

Hunting: Stocked pheasant, woodcock, grouse, waterfowl, raccoon, gray squirrel, cottontail, deer and black bear.
Fishing: Trout in the East Branch.

For further information contact: Headquarters, Wildlife District Manager, 400 Hubbard Ave., Pittsfield, MA 01201. ☎ (413) 447-9789.

Hiram H. Fox Wildlife Management Area

Location: Near Cummington off of SR 9.

The land is rolling with some steep ledges and gullies, elevations from 700 feet to 1,200 feet, forested with a mixture of hardwoods and conifers.

Wildlife: Black bear, wild turkey, grouse, deer, raccoon, snowshoe hare, gray squirrel, and bobcat.

For further information contact: Headquarters, Wildlife District Manager, 400 Hubbard Ave., Pittsfield, MA 01201. ☎ (413) 447-9789.

Hockomock Swamp Wildlife Management Area

Location: From SR 24, Exit 15.

Lake Nippenicket is at the southern corner of this wildlife area. Much of the area is wooded, but the main attraction is the wetlands: maple and cedar swamps, marshlands, open water and flowing streams. The best way to explore the area is by canoe.

Lake Nippenicket, 368 acres, was formerly owned by a hunting club. The lake has a boat ramp. Shore fishing, birding, and duck hunting opportunities are available along an unimproved road and foot trail on the west side.

Birds: Of the waterfowl, black duck, mallard, wood duck, and teal are most abundant. Other bird species include pheasant, grouse, woodcock, quail, and many songbirds.
Mammals: Includes deer, snowshoe hare, cottontail, squirrel, muskrat, fox, raccoon, mink, weasel, opossum, otter, skunk.
Fishing: Lake has chain pickerel, largemouth bass, black crappie.

Canoeing/Boating: The Town River flows north from Lake Nippenicket. The Town River, as well as the Snake River, and the lake are canoeable, although the segment of the Town River just beyond the lake is often overgrown.

For further information contact: Headquarters, Wildlife District Manager, 195 Boumedale Rd., Buzzards Bay, MA 02532. ☎ (508) 759-3406.

Hopkinton State Park

Location: From I-495, Exit 21 east to Hopkinton.

This is a day-use only park with water-based recreation. It is heavily used in warm weather, and complete with a recreation field, pavilion, boathouse, bathhouse, five launching ramps, and a dozen parking areas. The lake is surrounded by hardwood forest.

Hiking: A trail about one mile long traverses the north boundary of the site.

For further information contact: Headquarters, Hopkinton State Park, Cedar St., Hopkinton, MA 01748. ☎ (508) 435-4303.

Hubbardston Wildlife Management Area

Location: Central Massachusetts Route 202 to Route 68S.

The Metropolitan District Commission owns about 8,000 acres in this watershed, 1,000 of which are managed for wildlife. Uplands are open fields, brushy fields, and young forest. Excellent hunting in season and surprisingly good birding in the summer are some of the reasons to visit.

For further information contact: Headquarters, Wildlife District Manager, Temple St., West Boylston, MA 01583. ☎ (508) 835-3607.

John C. Phillips Wildlife Sanctuary/Boxford State Forest

Location: From Exit 51 on I-95, turn west. Take the first right (Middleton Rd.) about 1 mile to the parking area on left.

This sanctuary was donated to the state by a private citizen and is a jewel in the natural areas system of Massachusetts. The site is noted among birders for barred owl, pileated woodpecker, and Louisiana waterthrush, as well as many more common nesting species.

Wildflowers include lily-of-the-valley, Solomon's-seal, Indian pipe, pipsissewa, pink lady's-slipper.

For more information contact: Division of Fisheries and Wildlife, 100 Cambridge St., Boston, MA 02202. ☎ (617) 727-3180.

Kenneth Dubuque Memorial State Forest

(formerly Hawley State Forest)

Location: From Adams go 13 miles SE on SR 116, then N 1 mile on SR 8A.

This Forest has a well-developed trail system, with separate trails for hiking, horse riding, and recreation vehicles. It is one of the few parks where overnight stays are permitted.

The terrain of this park is heavily forested, rugged, with elevations from 1,200 to 2,000 feet. The site has several brooks, beaver dams, and two ponds. The forest is full of northern hardwoods with some white pine, hemlock, and spruce; azalea and hobblebush grow in the understory. Seasonal wildflowers include violets, adder's-tongue, orchids, trillium, touch-me-not, trout lily, spring beauty, gentians.

Birds: Include ruffed grouse, woodcock, hawks, owls, bluebird, scarlet tanager, thrushes, brown thrasher, flycatcher, black-capped chickadee, tufted titmouse, brown creeper, warblers, some waterfowl.
Mammals: Include snowshoe hare, cottontail, red and gray squirrels, fox, raccoon, skunk, muskrat, beaver, otter, mink, weasel, bobcat, deer. Occasional black bear and coyote.

Hiking/Backpacking: Eight miles of designated hiking trails; 35 miles of little-used woods roads, some overgrown.
Fishing: Ponds and streams. Trout, perch, pickerel.

For further information contact: Headquarters, Kenneth Dubuque Memorial State Park, Hawley, MA 01070. ☎ (413) 339-6631.

Leominster State Forest

Location: Near Fitchburg and Leominster from SR 2, about 2 miles on SR 31.

Terrain is rolling to steep, from a base elevation of about 800 feet. Most of it is forested with a mixture of hardwoods six to eight inches in diameter. White pine, blueberries, and wildflowers also grow rampant.

Oddly enough many of the trails in this state forest are used for cross-country motorcycle endurance runs. These runs do damage. The trails are often deeply rutted, muddy, and eroding. Many cyclists have ridden as much as 30 ft. off the trail, cutting raw gouges into the forest itself.

Hiking: 28 miles of trails, some steep.
Hunting: Deer and small upland game in undeveloped areas.
Fishing: Trout stocked in Crow Pond.
Swimming: Pond and stream.

For further information contact: Headquarters, Leominster State Forest, PO Box 32, East Princeton, MA 01517. ☎ (508) 874-2303.

Martha's Vineyard State Forest
Martin Burns Wildlife Management Area

Location: South of Newburyport between I-95 and US 1.

The land is gently rolling with many rock outcrops. Primary wildlife habitats are brush and young hardwood forest with small clearings, but there are also large areas of marsh and wooded swamp.

Wildlife: Most native species are present, including many song-birds. Pheasant and snowshoe hare are stocked.
Hunting: Special rules are posted. Read them carefully!

For further information contact: Headquarters, Wildlife District Manager, Harris St., Box 86, Acton, MA 01720. ☎ (508) 263-4347.

Millers River Wildlife Management Area

Location: From Athol take Route 202 to Peterborough, then drive W on Miller's River Rd.

The Birch Hill Flood Control Dam regulates river flow. Whitewater canoeists are attracted by Class III rapids during spring high water.

For further information contact: Headquarters, District Wildlife Manager, Temple St., West Boylston, MA 01583. ☎ (508) 835-3607.

Mohawk Trail State Forest

Location: On both sides of SR 2 about 18 miles east of North Adams.

This is a wonderful hiker's forest that offers a challenge to all. The adjacent Savoy has a more extensive trail system, but here there are also woods roads and paths worn by hunters and fishermen, or you can bushwhack. Except in hunting season, few people are in the backcountry.

Plants: Nearly 100% forested, mainly with beech, birches, maples, oaks on the southern slopes, scattered stands of hemlock, white pine, and spruce. Abundant mountain laurel, azalea, blueberries, raspberries, and wild roses. Seasonal wildflowers include bloodroot, Dutchman's-breeches, trout-lily, violets, orchids, trillium, gentians, lily-of-the-valley.
Birds: Many grouse, woodcock, hawks, owls, songbirds.
Mammals: Deer, black bear, bobcat, raccoon, skunk, red and gray squirrels, red and gray foxes, otter, snowshoe hare, cottontail, coyote, porcupine, fisher.
Camping: 56 sites on the Cold River.
Hiking: Trails to Clark Mountain and Todd Mountain.
Fishing: Good trout fishing in both rivers.

Canoeing: Whitewater on some sections of the Deerfield River.
Swimming: Beach near campground.

For further information contact: Headquarters, PO Box 7, Charlemont, MA 01339. ☎ (413) 339-5504.

Monomoy National Wildlife Refuge

*Location: An island at the bend of Cape Cod, accessible only by boat across a
mile-wide channel.*

Monomoy, a 10-mile-long barrier beach between Nantucket
Sound and the Atlantic Ocean, is a National Wilderness Area,
roadless and undeveloped with no visitor facilities. The island is
best known for its spring shorebirds.

The long, narrow island has sand beaches, dunes over 100 feet high,
salt and freshwater marshes, freshwater ponds, kettleholes, dense
thickets of scrub oak, pitch pine, black alder, and willow.

Birds: Nearly 300 species have been reported, 75 of them considered rare. Species nesting here include Canada goose, black duck,
piping plover, horned lark, savannah and sharp-tailed sparrows;
common, arctic, roseate, and least terns. Migrants include semi-
palmated and black-bellied plovers, ruddy turnstone whimbrel,
greater and lesser yellowlegs, red knot; pectoral, least, and semi-
palmated sandpipers; dunlin, sanderling, harlequin duck, king
eider, hooded merganser, bald eagle, osprey, peregrine falcon, Wilson's phalarope.
Mammals: Includes muskrat, mink, river otter, raccoon, longtail
weasel, deer, occasional harbor seal.
Hiking: Beach on Monomoy. Fantastic!
Fishing: Striped bass, bluefish, flounder.
Swimming: Surf. Be careful. There are no lifeguards.
Warning: Winds and rip tides often make the crossing to Monomoy
dangerous, especially during the winter months.

For further information contact: Headquarters, Monomy National
Wildlife Refuge, Morris Island, MA 02633. ☎ (617) 945-0594.

Monroe State Forest

Location: From North Adams, about 4 miles E on SR 2. Then 2 miles E on Tilda Hill Rd.

The terrain is mountainous, with steep slopes, rock ledges and outcrops, elevations from 1,700 to 2,730 ft. The Forest has no river frontage, but Raycroft Lookout overlooks the scenic river gorge. Dunbar Brook, which runs across the Forest, has numerous small falls and rapids.

The area is crowded with northern hardwoods; red spruce increases on upper slopes. Wildlife is typical of this region: deer, upland small game, many birds, and an occasional bear.

Camping: Only three hike-in sites.
Hiking: Nine miles of designated foot trails, plus numerous opportunities for those wishing to blaze their own trail.
Hunting: Deer, snowshoe hare, bobcat, raccoon, cottontail, squirrels, grouse, woodcock.
Fishing: Trout streams.

For further information contact: Headquarters, c/o Mohawk Trail State Forest, PO Box 7, Charlemont, MA 01339. ☎ (413) 339-5504.

Mt. Grace, Northfield, Warwick State Forests

Location: From Athol, W on SR 2 A; N on SR 78.

Trees in these forests include northern hardwoods with some white pine and hemlock. Mountain laurel and azalea are prominent in the understory, with trillium, lady's-slipper, mayflower, Solomon's-seal, and clintonia as common wildflowers. Birds and mammals are also typical of the region.

Northfield has several streams and small swamps. It is crossed by several gravel roads. Woods roads offer hiking opportunities. Snowmobilers may use the area in winter.

Mt. Grace attracts hikers because the Metacomet-Monadnock Trail crosses the summit. There is a shelter for backpackers on the Trail. Several brooks and springs.

For further information contact: Headquarters, Mt. Grace, North-field, Warwick State Forests, Warwick, MA 01264. ☎ (508) 544-7474.

Mt. Washington State Forest

Location: Southwest corner of MA. From south Egremont on SR 41 to Mt. Washington Rd.

The area is rugged, scenic, heavily forested, with steep slopes, rock outcrops, and ledges. Some of the nearby mountains are privately owned and inaccessible, but there is ample backcountry for hikers.

The main attraction for visitors to this state forest is Bash-Bish Falls, set in a spectacular gorge. The falls are most impressive during the spring runoff but are always scenic.

Camping: 15 hike-in sites. Always crowded during the summer months.
Hiking/Backpacking: The Appalachian Trail crosses Mt. Everett, heading south into Connecticut. A trailhead for Mt. Everett is at the Berkshire School off SR 41.

For further information contact: Headquarters, Mt. Washington State Forest, Mt. Washington, MA 01258. ☎ (413) 528-0330.

Myles Standish State Forest

Location: From I-495 near Plymouth, Exit 2. Go north on SR 68 to South Carver, then follow signs.

Just 40 miles outside of Boston, this state forest is always crowded, whether it be during the warm summer months or during the popular hunting seasons.

Plants: The Forest is home to some of the rarest plant species in the state. They are found throughout the Forest in two rare, natural communities: coastal plain pondshore, and pitch pine/scrub oak barrens. Ground cover includes blueberry, ferns, mushrooms, and wildflowers. Open fields have been planted with seed crops for birds.

Birds: Species include hawks, owls, whip-poor-wills, nighthawks, chickadees, juncos, titmouse, nuthatch sparrows, scarlet tanagers, bluebirds, northern orioles, cedar waxwings, woodpeckers, warblers, grosbeaks, marsh birds, and waterfowl.

Mammals: Red and gray foxes, red and gray squirrels, raccoon, cottontail, opossum, muskrat, mice, occasional deer.

Reptiles/Amphibians: Garter, black, grass, and hog-nosed snakes; box tortoise.

Camping: 475 sites in numerous campgrounds.

Hiking: Roads cross the area at intervals of about a half-mile, and these roads are used by horses, bicycles, and motorcycles. Hikers have no trails of their own.

Hunting: Pheasant and quail, grouse, rabbit deer.

Fishing: Bass, perch, pickerel, and trout in the ponds.

Swimming: Two sand-bottom ponds. Supervised in season.

For further information contact: Headquarters, PO Box 66, South Carver, MA 02366. ☎ (508) 866-2526.

Nickerson State Park

Location: Off SR 6A in East Brewster.

*C*liff Pond, at its center, is the largest of four ponds within the boundaries that offer swimming, boating, and fishing. The Park has an interpretive program, including an amphitheater.

Camping: 420 sites.

Hiking: Eight miles of trails link with the Cape Cod Rail Trail.

For further information contact: Headquarters, Nickerson State Park, Route 6A, Brewster, MA 02631. ☎ (508) 896-3491.

October Mountain State Forest

Location: From US 20 at Lenox or Lee.

*O*ne of the largest state forests lies across the Hoosac Range, just east of the Berkshire Valley. The region is rugged, scenic, and heavily forested, with many rock outcrops and ledges. The numerous streams draining the area drop over many falls and cataracts.

The largest of several ponds are 212-acre Lake Felton and 200-acre Finerty Pond. From Lake Felton, a swift brook rushes through Schermerhorn Gorge, emptying into the Housatonic River.

Plants: Mixed hardwoods, maples, oaks, and birches, with hemlock and spruce. Many flowering shrubs abide in the understory. Seasonal wildflowers include bloodroot, hepatica, jack-in-the-pulpit, wood and trout lilies, may-apple, lady's-slipper, trillium, rhodora, blue flag, and trailing arbutus.

Mammals: Deer, black bear, bobcat, coyote, red fox; red, gray, and flying squirrels; shorttail weasel, cottontail, snowshoe hare, muskrat, porcupine, beaver, fisher, raccoon, skunk, otter, deer, and white-footed mice.

Camping: 50 sites.

Hiking: 12 miles of trails, including the Appalachian Trail.

Fishing: Bass, pickerel, bullhead.

Boating: Ramp into Finerty Pond.

For further information contact: Headquarters, October Mountain State Forest, Woodlawn Rd., Lee, MA 01238. ☎ (413) 243-1778.

Oxbow National Wildlife Refuge

Location: Exit 29 from I-495.

This wildlife refuge was formerly a bombing range given to the state by the Department of Defense. Visitors are urged not to touch any unusual metallic objects. Uplands include a few pine-covered knolls. Several primitive trails cross the Refuge, one beside the river. The range of elevations is 210 to 250 ft.

Birds: The Refuge is maintained for migratory birds, notably black and wood ducks. Other waterfowl can be seen, as well as bittern, herons, snipe, sandpipers, woodcock, osprey, pheasant, and grouse.

Mammals: Species reported include woodchuck, snowshoe hare, red and gray squirrels, cottontail, raccoon, skunk, opossum, river otter, red fox, muskrat, deer.

Hunting: Special regulations posted during hunting season.

Fishing: Some chain pickerel and bullhead in the river.

Canoeing: Nashua River.

Ski touring: Trail map available from Fort Devens, Ayer, MA 01433.

For further information contact: Headquarters, Great Meadows National Wildlife Refuge, Weir Hill, Sudbury, MA 01776. ☎ (508) 443-4661.

Peru Wildlife Management Area

Location: East of Peru on SR 143.

*T*rout Brook crosses the area north to south. The site is almost totally forested with a mix of northern hardwoods and conifers.

Wildlife includes grouse, woodcock, snowshoe hare, raccoon, beaver, black bear, bobcat, and deer. The brook has a good number of trout.

For further information contact: Wildlife District Manager, 400 Hubbard Ave., Pittsfield, MA 01201. ☎ (413) 447-9789.

Phillipston Wildlife Management Area

Location: Begin in Athol, then bear south on SR 32 to SR 101.

Hunting: Stocked with snowshoe hare. Game species include deer, turkey, grouse, cottontail, woodcock, and pheasant. Some waterfowl use the marshy areas.
Fishing: Trout in several streams.

For further information contact: Headquarters, Wildlife District Manager, Temple St., West Boylston, MA 01583. ☎ (508) 835-3607.

Pittsfield State Forest

Location: Just outside of Pittsfield.

*N*o one can argue that this isn't a hiker's forest. The Taconic Skyline Trail runs the entire length of the ridge, passing Berry Pond. More than a dozen trails ascend from the east side. Slopes are moderate to steep, with rock outcrops, ledges, and caves. Deer and bear are often seen.

Camping: 31 sites.
Hiking: 30 miles of good trails.
Fishing: Berry Pond is stocked.

For further information contact: Pittsfield State Forest, Cascade St., Pittsfield, MA 01201. ☎ (413) 442-8992.

Quaboag Wildlife Management Area

Location: 20 miles west of Worcester.

Much of the site is freshwater marsh along the Quaboag River. The river and wetlands attract osprey, American bittern, long-billed marsh wren, sandpipers, egrets, and herons.

The river is navigable for canoes, usually all year, with slow-moving flatwater. There is no established put-in or take-out in this wildlife management area. Downstream is a 103-mile stretch of rapids ranging from Class II to Class IV.

Hiking: Three miles of roads and trails.
Hunting: Deer, squirrel, cottontail, and native waterfowl.
Fishing: Pike, largemouth bass, and panfish.

For further information contact: Headquarters, District Wildlife Manager, Temple St., West Boylston, MA 01583. ☎ (508) 835-3607.

Sandisfield State Forest

Location: SR 57 near Sandisfield.

The terrain of this forest is hilly, with brooks, streams, and swamps, and a diverse wildlife population. Included within the forest boundaries are 20 miles of hiking trails and 10 "wilderness" campsites.

There is fishing and hiking but, oddly, no hunting – a little unusual when compared to other state forests in Massachusetts.

For further information contact: Headquarters, West St., Sandisfield, MA 01255. ☎ (413) 258-4774.

Savoy Mountain State Forest

Location: 5 miles east of North Adams on SR 2.

The terrain of this state forest is rugged to mountainous with elevations from 1,800 ft. to 2,566 ft. The area has many streams, waterfalls, and several ponds, the largest of which is 40 acres. Scenic trails take you up the two peaks and lead to such points of interest as North Pond, Balanced Rocks, Crooked Forest, and 80 ft. Tannery Falls.

Plants: About 80% forested with mixed hardwoods. Increasing amounts of spruce, fir, and pine at high elevations. Understory of striped maple, mountain laurel, raspberry, blackberry, and fireweed. Some reverting fields are found. Spring wildflower displays. Some boggy areas have typical wetland species. Crooked Forest has trees presumably deformed by an ice storm years ago.

Birds: No checklist or reports of observations other than hawks migrating in the fall.

Mammals: Deer, bear, snowshoe hare, cottontail, porcupine, fisher, red and gray squirrels, red and gray foxes, and woodchuck.

Camping: 45 sites.

Hiking: 24 miles of trails.

Fishing: Trout in streams and ponds.

Swimming: South Pond and North Pond.

For further information contact: Headquarters, Savoy Mountain State Forest, RFD # 2, North Adams, MA 01247. ☎ (413) 662-8469.

Tolland State Forest

Location: From Lee, E about 7 miles on US Route 20 to junction with SR 8 in West Becket.

The Forest lies between SR 8 and the south end of Otis Reservoir. The campground, beach, and boat ramp are at the north end of the Forest on a peninsula that divides Southwest Bay from the main body of water. Between the dam and the campground entrance, a paved road runs south to the Forest boundary. No signs are visible identifying forest land from surrounding area.

The area covered by the map (available at the information booth) is rolling to hilly, forested, with a moderate understory. State headquarters mentions a 310-acre Big Pond (evidently beyond the map's scope), rivers, streams, and a waterfall.

Birds: Hawks: Cooper's, redtailed, goshawk, and sharp-shinned. Owls: barred, great horned, long-eared, short-eared, screech, and saw-whet. Great blue herons, American bitterns, common loons, gulls, black skimmers, ospreys, belted kingfishers, northern orioles, brown creepers, cedar waxwings, cardinals, purple finches, American goldfinches; evening, pine, and rose-breasted grosbeaks; bank, barn, and cliff swallows; woodpeckers, ruby-throated hummingbirds, many warblers and sparrows, chimney swifts.
Mammals: Include red and gray foxes, beaver, bobcat, muskrat, otter, weasel, mink, skunk, snowshoe hare, cottontail, chipmunks; red, gray, and flying squirrels, and deer.
Camping: 90 sites, 35 on the shore.
Hiking: 10 miles of multi-purpose trails bordering reservoir.
Hunting: Deer, small game, and turkey.
Fishing: Trout, bass, bluegill, white and yellow perch, pickerel.
Swimming: Beach near camping area.
Boating: Ramp near camping area. No horsepower limit.

For further information contact: Headquarters, Tolland State Forest, Otis, MA 01008. ☎ (413) 269-7268.

Upton State Forest

Location: From I-495, take Exit 21 and head northeast to SR 135 in Hopkinton, then to SR 135. Turn left on Spring St. and go 2 miles to Westboro Rd.

The site offers an opportunity for pleasantly quiet woodland hiking when most sites near Boston are crowded. Off-road vehicles are permitted.

Hiking: Six miles of trails in two loops.

For more information contact: Mass. Division of Forests and Parks, 100 Cambridge St., Boston, MA 02202. ☎ (617) 727-3180.

Wachusett Meadow Wildlife Sanctuary

Location: One hour west of Boston on Mountain Rd. in Princeton.

A large sanctuary, this adjoins the 1,950-acre Wachusett Mountain State Reservation and is linked to it and other State properties by the Mid-State Trail.

Plants: Species include red oak, white pine, hemlock, sugar maple, white ash, black cherry, beech, birch, and basswood. An understory includes hophornbeam and blueberry. The Crocker maple is one of the largest of its species in North America, over 300 years old. Woodlands include a hemlock ravine, a stand of shagbark hickory, and dark groves of hemlock and beech.

Wildflowers: Prominent are foamflower, painted trillium, three-toothed cinquefoil, dwarf ginseng, wood anemone, and marsh marigold.

Birds: Ovenbird, red-eyed vireo, common yellowthroat, blue jay, American robin, tree swallow, black-capped chickadee, red-winged blackbird, and cliff swallow. Take advantage of an excellent opportunity to view the fall migration of hawks, peaking in mid-Sept. The best birding season is May to mid-June.

Mammals: Shorttail shrews, big brown bats, white-footed mice, redback and meadow voles, porcupines, woodchucks, chipmunks, red and gray squirrels, snowshoe hares, cottontails, raccoons, weasels, skunks, red and gray foxes, and deer.

Hiking: 11 miles of trails. The Mid-State Trail, Rhode Island to New Hampshire, crosses the site.

For further information contact: Headquarters, Wachusett Meadow Wildlife Sanctuary, PO Box 268, Princeton, MA 01541. ☎ (508) 464-2712.

Walden Pond State Reservation

Location: From SR 2 in Concord, S on SR 126.

Hike the trails where Henry David Thoreau spent time. These gorgeous trails are extremely popular; on pleasant weekends the thousand-car parking lot isn't sufficient.

For further information contact: Massachusetts Division of Forests and Parks, 100 Cambridge St., Boston, MA 02202. ☎ (617) 727-3180.

Wendell State Forest

Location: 12 miles east on SR 2 to Millers Falls.

The area is rolling to hilly, less mountainous than nearby forests. The woodland is home to oak and sugar maple as well as some hemlock and white pine. Ruggles Pond and Wickett Pond are within the Forest; Bowens Pond is just outside.

Hiking: On the Metacomet-Monadnock Trail.
Hunting: Deer, woodcock, turkey, grouse, rabbit, bobcat, and raccoon.
Fishing: Trout in streams. Bass, perch.
Swimming: Ruggles Pond.
Canoeing: Canoeing available on Millers River.

For further information contact: Headquarters, Wendell State Forest, RFD 1, Wendell Rd., Millers Falls, MA 01349. ☎ (413) 659-3797.

Willard Brook State Forest

Location: North about 6 miles from Fitchburg.

The site is hilly with rock ledges, forested with an understory of shrubs, ferns, and wildflowers.

Picnicking: Sites are distributed along the brook.
Camping: 21 sites at Damon Pond and an additional 51 sites at Pearl Hill.
Hiking: 18 miles of trails.
Hunting: Small upland game.
Fishing: Trout stocked.
Swimming: Pearl Hill Pond (five acres) and Damon Pond (two acres).

For further information contact: Headquarters, Townsend, MA 01469. ☎ (508) 597-8802.

Willowdale State Forest

Location: From US 1 in Ipswich, 3.6 miles north of SR 97.

 $\mathcal{T}$ he most appealing feature of this state forest is Willowdale Swamp. Several brooks drain to the Ipswich River. Highest point is 194-ft. Bartholomew Hill.

Fortunately for hikers off-road vehicles are prohibited, which makes for quiet hiking. The diversity of habitats attracts a variety of wildlife. Birding is fabulous!

Hiking: Chiefly on old woods roads and upland surrounding the swamp.

For further information contact: Headquarters, Massachusetts Division of Forests and Parks, 100 Cambridge St., Boston, MA 02202. ☎ (617) 727-3180.

Wompatuck State Park

Location: About 20 miles southeast of Boston.

 $\mathcal{W}$ hat more could a city dweller ask for? This state park is near Boston and the coast, and it has one of the state's largest campgrounds. Sorry – there is no swimming available, but the wonders of nature will bring you back time and time again.

Plants: Forest Sanctuary Climax Grove has large white pine, hemlock, and American beech, some specimens more than 180 years old. Other tree species in the Park include red pine, elm, white oak, sweet birch, Norway maple, and white ash. Understory species include holly, swamp azalea, and sheep laurel.
Wildlife: Bird species include pheasant, grouse, goshawks, owls, northern harriers, green herons, quails, and many songbirds. Mammals include cottontails, raccoons, skunks, and muskrats.
Camping: 400 sites.
Hiking: 10 miles of trails.
Hunting: Pheasant, grouse, cottontail.
Ski touring: 10 miles of trails.

For further information contact: The Superintendent, Wompatuck State Park, Union St., Hingham, MA 02043. ☎ (617) 749-7160.

National Sites

Cape Cod National Seashore

*M*ention Cape Cod and people think of many things: swimming and sunbathing, fishing and whaling, clams and cranberries, writers and artists, cottages and shops, Pilgrims and Indians. All are part of the ambiance and charm that attract thousands of visitors to the Cape each year. To help protect the special qualities of this environment, the National Seashore was established in 1961 in the 40-mile-long section between Chatham and Provincetown. Each of the National Park Service sites within this area tells a part of the Cape Cod story.

The Cape is a glacial deposit that is constantly undergoing natural changes as the winds and water drive sand along the shorelines, tearing away one place and building another. An example of how quickly the land is diminishing is evident at the Marconi Wireless Station site at Wellfeet, where the peninsula is only a mile wide. Much of the high cliff has eroded since Guglielmo Marconi first built his towers there in 1901. Changing, too, though not so perceptibly, is the Cape Cod Bay shoreline. Great Island, where whalers used to congregate, is now connected to the peninsula; you can explore it via a trail.

The Cape's human history is just as rich as its natural history. In the Provincetown area you can see where the Pilgrims landed in 1620 before sailing across the bay to Plymouth. At the National Seashore there are several historic buildings that reflect the residents' longtime association with the sea. The Old Harbor Lifesaving Station was moved in two pieces from Chatham to Race Point near Provincetown in 1977; Captain Edward Penniman's 1868 house in Eastham is atypically ornate but denotes the once profitable whaling business; Nauset Light is one of the five lighthouses within the Seashore; and the Atwood-Higgins House, built about 1730, represents the typical Cape Cod dwelling. Most of these structures are open for tours in the summer. Inquire at the visitor center.

Recreation and Relaxation

Cape Cod National Seashore offers a variety of land and water recreational activities that can be as relaxing and soul-restoring as you let them be. Take time to try something different, whether it be bicycling or hiking or just sitting by the ocean watching the waves. For further information, ask for a schedule at the visitor center.

Activities

Swimming: Seasonal lifeguard services and other related facilities are located at these beaches: Coast Guard, Nauset Light, Marconi, Head of the Meadow, Race Point, and Herring Cove. Several towns also have public beaches; all charge fees. Please observe water safety practices at all times.

Surfing/Windsurfing: Within the National Seashore surfing is permitted in waters outside lifeguarded beaches.

Walks: The Seashore has a number of short self-guiding trails. We invite you to walk them to relax and to gain an insight into the Cape's natural and human history. Perhaps their descriptive names will entice you: Fort Hill, Red Maple Swamp, Nauset Marsh, Great Island, Pamet Cranberry Bog, Atlantic White Cedar Swamp, Small Swamp, Pilgrim Spring, and Beech Forest. Brochures about each trail may be obtained at the visitor centers. Buttonbush Trail, with special features for the blind, starts at Salt Pond Visitor Center.

Bicycling: The Seashore maintains three bicycle trails ranging from 1.6 to 7.3 miles. Roller-skating, skateboarding, and the use of motorized vehicles, including mopeds, on these paved trails are prohibited. Bicycles may be rented within the towns.

Fishing: Try surf-fishing from the many beaches, but stay away from swimmers. No license is required for saltwater fishing, but a state license is required for freshwater fishing. Town licenses for shellfishing are required. Regulations and fees vary.

Hunting: Upland game and migratory waterfowl may be hunted in certain areas in the specified season. There is no open season on non-game species. Ask for a brochure on hunting opportunities and restrictions. Federal, state, and local laws apply.

Headquarters: The National Seashore is administered by the National Park Service, US Department of the Interior. The Seashore headquarters is located near Marconi Station site. For park information, send a stamped, self-addressed, business-size envelope to:

Superintendent, Cape Cod National Seashore, South Wellfleet, MA 02663. ☎ (508) 349-3785.

Cape Cod Self-Guiding Nature Trails

Eastham Trails

Fort Hill Trail (includes the Red Maple Swamp)
Length: 1½ miles. Allow at least an hour for entire walk.
Access: Turn left (east) at Fort Hill sign on Governor Prence Road. Continue on Fort Hill Road a quarter mile to parking area on left, across from Captain Edward Penniman House.
Moderate walking difficulty, solid surface. Some log steps on slopes. Tree roots in Red Maple Swamp protrude above ground. Part of this trail is boardwalk.

ButtonBush Trail
Length: ¼ mile.
Access: Near Salt Pond Visitor Center amphitheater. Trail begins where you see the sign and white guide rope.
Special Features: Texts in Braille and large print; guide rope.
Easy; some log steps, moderate grade. Part of this trail is boardwalk.

Nauset Marsh Trail
Length: One mile.
Access: Outside the Salt Pond Visitor Center to the right of the outdoor amphitheater. Trail winds along edge of Salt Pond and Nauset Marsh, crosses field and returns to Visitor Center. Be careful when crossing bicycle trail.
Easy; some log steps, moderate grade.

Wellfleet Trails

Atlantic White Cedar Swamp Trail
Length: 1¼ miles.
Access: Turn right (east) into Marconi Station Area at traffic light on US Highway 6, South Wellfleet, 5¼ miles north of Salt Pond Visitor Center, Eastham. Follow signs to Marconi Site and White Cedar Swamp, at end of road, one mile past park headquarters.

Moderate difficulty; some steep stairs. Return route is ½ mile in soft sand. Part of this trail is boardwalk.

Great Island Trail
Length: Four miles, one way.
Access: At traffic light on US Highway 6, turn left (west) into Wellfleet center; left again onto Commercial Street. Turn right at town pier, onto Kendrick Road, and left onto Chequesset Neck Road. Trail begins at Great Island parking lot, 3½ miles from traffic light on US Highway 6. Head covering, sturdy footgear and drinking water are advisable.

The National Seashore's most difficult trail; most soft sand. Some log steps.

Truro Trails

Cranberry Bog Trail
Length: ½ mile.
Access: Turn right (east) on North Pamet Road, Truro. Proceed 1½ miles. Trail begins at the parking lot below the Environmental Education Center (a Youth Hostel in the summer).
Easy; some log steps, moderate grade. Part of this trail is boardwalk.

Small Swamp Trail
Length: ¾ mile.
Access: Turn right (east) at the Pilgrim Heights area sign. Walk begins at interpretive shelter.
Easy; many log steps, steep grade.

Pilgrim Spring Trail
Length: ¾ mile.
Access: Interpretive shelter, Pilgrim Heights area. Path leads to site of spring where Pilgrims may have drunk their first water in New England.
Easy; some log steps, moderate grade.

Provincetown Trail

Beech Forest Trail
Length: One mile.
Access: Turn right (north) at traffic light on Race Point Road. Proceed about half a mile to the Beech Forest parking log on the left side of the road.
More difficult; steep log steps, mostly soft sand.

Cape Cod Bike Trails

Distance:
- Loop Trail: 5¼ miles.
- Herring Cove Beach spur; one mile.
- Race Point Beach spur: ½ mile.
- Bennett Pond spur: ¼ mile.
- Race Point Road spur: ¼ mile.

Access points:
- Beech Forest Parking Area
- Province Lands Visitor Center
- Race Point Beach Parking Area
- Herring Cove Beach Parking Area
- Race Point Road near Provincetown

Lowell National Historical Park

Lowell National Historical Park commemorates Lowell, Massachusetts as the cradle of the American Industrial Revolution. Established in 1978, the park contains historic cotton textile mills, 5.6 miles of canals, and worker housing. Restored turn-of-the-century trolleys operate year-round as transportation for visitors touring the park. The Boott Cotton Mills Museum features a 1920s-era factory weave room filled with operating power looms and dynamic exhibits telling the story of industrialization. Other major facilities: the Visitor Center at Market Mills, the Working People Exhibit at the Morgan Cultural Center, the Suffolk Mill Turbine Exhibit, and the Lowell Heritage State Park's Waterpower Exhibit.

Visitor Center at Market Mills

Visit at Market Mills, the former Lowell Manufacturing Company mill complex, one of the city's original textile mills. Market Mills houses the National Park Visitor Center, where you can make reservations for tours, explore exhibits and view the award-winning slide show, *Lowell: The Industrial Revelation*. General information on area lodging and dining is also available. Open daily, 9 am to 5 pm. Free.

Also in Market Mills: The Visitor Center Bookstore; The Brush Art Gallery and Studios; and the Park Cafe and Gallery.

Weave Room

Trace the footsteps of mill workers as you enter the Boott Cotton Mills Museum and encounter a weave room of the early twentieth century. Weave rooms of this period would typically have had more looms, greater noise, much heat and humidity and air filled with cotton dust.

From 1896 to 1904, Boott Mills purchased over 1,100 looms of various models from the Draper Corporation of Hopedale, Massachusetts. The 88 looms in this room are Draper Model E's that first saw use in Fall River, Massachusetts, later shipped and used in a mill in Tennessee, then purchased in 1990 by the National Park Service and restored for this exhibit.

In Lowell and other New England mill towns, thousands of looms produced by such companies as the Lowell Machine Shop and the Draper Corporation, produced millions of yards of all types of cotton cloth each year.

When Boott first opened in the late 1830's, each weaver tended two looms. A century later, changes in technology made it possible for management to spread out their work force and assign 20 looms to each weaver. Laboring 10 to 12 hours each day, first the Yankee "mill girls" and later immigrants from many ethnic backgrounds endured the most difficult conditions of the mills. Their labors fueled America's Industrial Revolution and made the city of Lowell world-famous.

As you leave the weave room, proceed to the second floor of the exhibit to learn more of Lowell's place in America's industrialization.

Daily guided walking tours and summertime canal boat tours offer a unique look at Lowell's industrial landscape. The Park is open daily except Thanksgiving, Christmas, and New Year's. For more information contact: Lowell National Historic Park, 246 Market Street, Lowell, Massachusetts 01852. ☎ (508) 970-5000 (V/TDD).

Exploring Lowell

Programs to suit a variety of interests! Tour the Suffolk Mill and see a working 19th-century turbine and power loom. Explore the city's past through an architectural tour of the historic district. Learn about Lowell's early connection to patent medicine. These 60- to 90-minute programs or walking tours, focusing on various topics, begin at the Visitor Center daily at 2:30 pm. Call or ask a ranger for information on specific topics. Free.

Directions

To drive to Lowell National Historical Park take the Lowell Connector from either Route 495 (Exit 36) or Route 3 (Exit 30N) to Thorndike Street (Exit 5N). Follow brown and white "Lowell National and State Park" signs. Free parking is available at the Visitor Parking Lot next to Market Mills.

Parker River National Wildlife Refuge

Location: On Plum Island. From Newburyport on SR 1A, E on Water Street and Plum Island Turnpike, following signs.

There is no refuge quite like it. It includes six miles of splendid barrier shoreline. Crowds of visitors come just to enjoy the beach. Maps and leaflets are dispersed at the front gate. Be sure to arrive early since the refuge is an extremely popular site. 400,000 people visit the Refuge annually, most of them in summer. A five-dollar-per-car admission fee is applicable; annual passes are available.

The gate is at the north end of the Refuge. At the southern tip of the island is a small tract called Sandy Point State Park, administered as part of the Refuge. Seven parking areas are spaced along the road. Beach access is by boardwalk from six of them. Four-wheel-drive and off-road vehicles are allowed on the beach by permit.

Beach and fore-dunes are barren. Rear dunes, up to 50 ft. high, are heavily vegetated. On the inland side of the road, dikes have created several freshwater marshes and pools. Beyond are 3,200 acres of salt marsh and tidewater. These wetlands can be observed from dikes and a nature trail. Other habitats include glaciated uplands with goose pasture and wooded patches, and small glacial drumlins (a long, narrow rounded hill of unstratified glacial drift).

Hellcat Swamp Wildlife Trail: The trail begins at parking lot four (where there is no beach access). About two miles, with spurs and boardwalk, visits dunes, freshwater swamp, and a salt marsh. Observation tower. Trail guide available.

Plants: Species seen along the nature trail include blueberry, green-brier grape, chokecherry, blackberry, pin and black cherry, wood-bine, raspberry, honeysuckle, bayberry, poison ivy, beach plum, cranberry, spirea, speckled alder, willow, trembling aspen, dune grass, serviceberry, arrowwood, winter berry, cedar, staghorn su-mac, wild rose, and honeysuckle.

Birds: Checklist records 301 species plus 33 accidentals. The Refuge is along major bird migration routes. Salt marshes are important feeding and resting areas. Peak concentrations of up to 25,000 ducks and 6,000 geese occur in spring and fall. Other habitats attract large flocks of warblers and shorebirds.

Mammals: Species often seen include cottontail, fox, skunk, wea-sel, muskrat, harbor seal, woodchuck, and deer. Woodchucks emerge from hibernation March through April. Red fox kits are sometimes seen on roads at dawn or dusk in June and July.

Other Fauna: Monarch butterflies migrate through the Refuge in September.

Hiking: Six miles of fine beach. Two miles of nature trails, two miles of dikes. At the south end there are trails around the goose browse fields.

Hunting: In designated area. Special regulations. Inquire at head-quarters.

Fishing: Ocean beach, daylight hours, except a northern portion that is closed to fishing May through mid-October. Headquarters has a fishing leaflet with information on night access and vehicle permits.

Swimming: No lifeguards. Relatively cold water, rough surf, strong tides, undertow.

Boating: Launching or landing on the Refuge is prohibited except as specified in waterfowl hunting regulations. Boating in tidewater is governed by State and local regulations.

For further information contact: Headquarters, Parker River National Wildlife Refuge, Northern Blvd., Plum Island, Newburyport, MA 01950. ☎ (508) 465-5753.

New

Hampshire

State Parks

$\mathcal{N}$ew Hampshire is proud of its state parks; historic sites, nature areas and trails, the crystal clear waters, litter-free landscapes, crisp, clean mountain air, and rich cultural heritage. All add to the New Hampshire park experience. There are approximately 50,000 acres of public lands for recreation use that includes state parks, historic sites and forest, and 6,000 miles of trails woven through the state. Whether it's sunbathing and swimming, hiking, mountain biking or camping - it's all here.

Information on parks and recreation can be obtained from:

New Hampshire Division of Parks and Recreation
172 Pembroke Road
PO Box 856
Concord, NH 03302-0856
☎ (603) 271-3254

Androscoggin River

Location: From Errol to Berlin, beside SR 16.

With rapids of Class II and III and a relatively long season, this is one of New Hampshire's most popular canoe runs. The shoreline is relatively undeveloped, but there's little public land along the route. It is 35 river miles long.

For more information contact: Audubon Society of NH, PO Box 528-B, Concord, NH 03301. ☎ (603) 224-9909.

Annett State Forest

Location: From US 202 at Jaffrey,
south following signs just past Squantum.

The Forest includes more than half of the shoreline of Hubbard Pond, an odd-shaped water body about 1¼ miles in length. Hubbard Pond Road intersects the Forest, giving guests a sampling of typical New Hampshire terrains – flat to rolling land, second-growth northern hardwoods with some pine and hemlock.

Facilities: Hiking on old woods roads, hunting for deer and other select small game, and challenging fishing for smallmouth bass, pickerel, bullhead, and yellow perch.

For further information contact : Forest Headquarters, 105 Loudon Rd., Concord, NH 03301. ☎ (603) 271-2214.

Bear Brook State Park

Location: From Manchester, north on US 3, then north on SR 28. Signs.

The principal recreation area on Catamount Pond can accommodate 1,500 visitors in the picnic area, more on the beach and in the popular play areas. It's crowded in good weather and often difficult to find a spot to relax. Take note, however, the trail system is extensive, and relatively few visitors venture beyond the developed area.

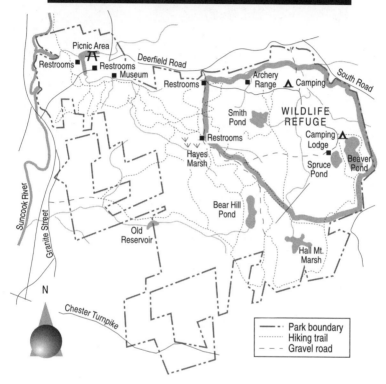

The terrain of this state park is rolling to steep. The elevation of Bear Hill is 800 ft. and, about 400 ft. above its base in the southern end of the park, Hall Mountain rises to 925 ft. The area is heavily wooded. Bear Brook flows north from Hall Mountain Marsh. There are five ponds, in addition to Catamount, and a number of small streams.

Camping: Over 80 tent sites available for campers mid-May to mid-October. The camping area is reserved for campers and has its own beach.

Hiking: Over 30 miles of hiking trails. Bear Brook's over 30 miles of trails, leading to seldom-visited marshes, bogs, summits and ponds, offer a variety of options for hikers, mountain bikers, and equestrians.

Hunting: Deer and other small game.
Swimming: Supervised beach.
Canoeing: Available.
Fishing: Brook trout and panfish. Fishing is so popular that one pond is reserved for fly fishing.

Two very popular hikes are the 1½-mile loop trail around Beaver Pond which begins and ends at the campground, and the short hike to Smith Pond. The Broken Boulder Trail, which crosses the campground just past (south) Archery Pond, leads to Smith Pond. The bog at Smith Pond makes it an especially interesting destination.

For futher information contact: Park Headquarters, Suncook, NH 03275. ☎ (603) 485-9874.

Charles L. Peirce Wildlife & Forest Reservation

Location: From SR 9 in Stoddard, 2 miles north on SR 123. Turn right at fire station. Turn right and follow the unpaved road for about ¾ of a mile.

This park was donated to the Society for the Protection of New Hampshire in 1978 as a memorial to Charles L. Peirce, a teacher and historian. This massive park covers 3,461 acres. It is reserved mainly for wildlife observation and hiking (over 10 miles of trails).

For further information contact: Forest Headquarters, Society for the Protection of New Hampshire Forests, 54 Portsmouth St., Concord, NH 03301. ☎ (603) 224-9945.

Coleman State Park

Location: At Colebrook, 6 miles east on SR 26 to Kidderville, then north for about 5-5 ½ miles.

Hikers and backpackers will love Northern New Hampshire – the terrain is largely mountainous, rugged, and basically without roads, except for logging trails. Coleman is on Little Diamond Pond, in the spruce-fir country, surrounded by near-perfect wilderness.

Snowmobilers will delight in the extensive network of snowmobile trails on timber company land. The distances between roads or settlements are great. Snows are usually deep, winters cold and windy. One section of the Androscoggin Trail crosses the Park, a route covering nearly 50 miles. There are no marked trails in this area, but the woods call to the adventurous.

Activities/Facilities: 30 tent sites; fishing for trout; boating (with horsepower and speed restrictions).

For further information contact: Park Headquarters, RFD 1, Colebrook, NH 03576.

Connecticut Lakes State Forest

*Location: Off of US 3 for about 10 miles,
just south of the Quebec boundary.*

The Audubon Society of New Hampshire considers this a prime birding area, especially for Canadian Zone species. Sighted species include black-backed and northern three-toed wood-peckers, spruce grouse, woodcocks, saw-whet owls, common ravens; Philadelphia, vireo, Trail's and yellow-bellied flycatchers; boreal, chickadee, red-breasted nuthatch, crossbills, purple finch, goldfinch, pine siskin, evening grosbeak, Swainson s thrush, swamp sparrow, gray jay, ruby-crowned and golden-crowned kinglets. Warblers: Tennessee, Wilson's, yellow-rumped, parula, magnolia, bay-breasted mourning. On the lakes birdwatchers will marvel at the common loons, ring-necked ducks, and goldeneye mergansers.

First Connecticut Lake: 2,807 acres, has a 19 mile undeveloped shoreline in near-wilderness that offers some of the best trout and salmon fishing in the country.
Second Connecticut Lake: 1,286 acres, 11 miles of wooded shoreline. Offers good trout and salmon fishing.
Third Connecticut Lake: 278 acres, at the Quebec border, is a natural body; not dammed. Note: launch site but no ramp.

For further information contact: Division of Parks and Recreation, PO Box 856D, Concord, NH 03301. ☎ (603) 271-3254.

Crawford Notch State Park

Location: On US 302, 12 miles north of Bartlett.

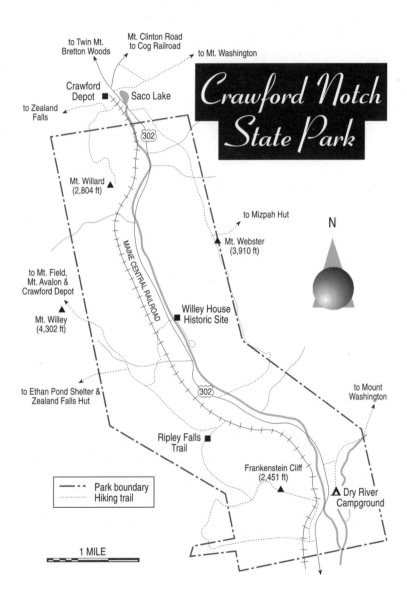

to Twin Mt.
Bretton Woods

Mt. Clinton Road
to Cog Railroad

to Mt. Washington

Crawford
Depot

Saco Lake

to Zealand
Falls

Crawford Notch State Park

302

Mt. Willard
(2,804 ft)

to Mizpah Hut

Mt. Webster
(3,910 ft)

N

to Mt. Field,
Mt. Avalon &
Crawford Depot

MAINE CENTRAL RAILROAD

Mt. Willey
(4,302 ft)

Willey House
Historic Site

to Ethan Pond Shelter &
Zealand Falls Hut

302

to Mount
Washington

Ripley Falls
Trail

Frankenstein Cliff
(2,451 ft)

Dry River
Campground

— · — Park boundary
········· Hiking trail

1 MILE

*M*ost of the land in the Crawford Notch was acquired by New Hampshire in 1913. It was the result of a bill passed by the legislature in 1922 aimed at rescuing the northern region of Hart's Location from excessive timber harvest. The bill failed to include the northern, most scenic part of the notch, which the state purchased in 1912 for $62,000. Almost 6,000 acres of land extends on both sides of the highway to the summits of the mountains that border the Saco River Valley. In 1922 the Willey House clearing was leased to Donahue and Hamlin of Bartlett who built a cabin colony of peeled spruce logs for vacationers. More log buildings were added, including restrooms and a restaurant and gift shop, but eventually the state took back the clearing for its own operations.

This six-mile mountain pass through some of the most rugged terrain of the White Mountains has been a well-traveled route since stagecoach days. The scenic 1½-mile-wide strip is surrounded by the White Mountain National Forest. The Notch is at 1,773-ft. elevation. Several nearby peaks are well above 3,700 ft., still higher ones not far off. The Appalachian Trail crosses the Park, and other trails lead to points of interest.

Camping: 30-35 tent sites.
Fishing: Nearby trout streams.
Hiking: A short nature trail is located just outside the park office.

For further information contact: Park Headquarters, Star Route, Bartlett, NH 03812. ☎ (603) 374-2272.

Echo Lake State Park

Location: From North Conway on US 302 and west on River Rd.

*T*his day-use park is open weekends beginning on Memorial Day, daily from late June to Labor Day. Most visitors come to picnic and swim, but there are some enticing hiking trails around the lake and up to Cathedral and White Horse ledges.

For further information contact: NH Division of Parks & Recreation, 105 Loudon Rd., Concord, NH 03301. ☎ (603) 271-3254.

Fox Forest

Location: From US 202 at Hillsborough, northwest on SR 107. Signs on the road will direct you.

In 1922 Caroline A. Fox donated the original 348 acres and established a trust fund that has supported a continuing program of research and education. The area is hilly and moderately rugged. Much of it was open farmland in the 1930s. Most of the site is again forested. Some portions of the original forest remain untouched. The site has over 20 miles of trails.

Plants: Native trees: white, red, and pitch pine; red and black spruce; balsam fir; eastern red cedar; tamarack; eastern hemlock. Hardwoods: black willow; trembling and large-toothed aspen; butternut; shagbark hickory; black, yellow, paper, and gray birch; speckled alder; red and white oak; sugar, red, and striped maple.
Birds: Around buildings, shade trees, and orchards: rock and mourning doves, ruby-throated hummingbirds, yellow-bellied sapsuckers, hairy and downy wood-peckers, eastern phoebes, eastern wood-pewees, tree and barn swallows, black-capped chickadees, tufted titmouse, white-breasted nuthatches, house wrens, American robins, eastern bluebirds, red-eyed and warbling vireos, house sparrows, northern orioles, rose-breasted grosbeaks, purple finches, and chipping sparrows. Freshwater marshes, swamps, and bogs: pied-billed grebes, great blue herons.
Mammals: Snowshoe hare, red and gray squirrels, chipmunk, fox, porcupine, raccoon, beaver, skunk, otter, muskrat, mink, whitetail deer, and an occasional bobcat.

For further information contact: Forest Headquarters, Hillsboro, NH 03244. ☎ (603) 464-3453.

Franconia Notch State Park

Location: On I-93 just south of Franconia.

The eight-mile-long pass between the peaks of the Franconia and Kinsman ranges is one of the most incredible areas in the White Mountains. It is also one of the busiest. It is surrounded by the White Mountain National Forest, and numerous trails offer routes to places of quiet beauty.

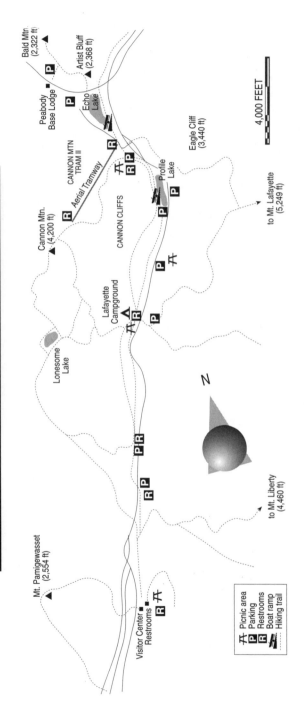

Franconia Notch State Park

Bald Mtn.
(2,322 ft) ▲

Artist Bluff
(2,368 ft) ▲

Peabody
Base Lodge ■ P

Echo
Lake

Eagle Cliff
(3,440 ft)

CANNON MTN
TRAM II

R

Aerial Tramway

Profile
Lake

P
R P

CANNON CLIFFS

Cannon Mtn.
(4,200 ft) ▲

R

P

to Mt. Lafayette
(5,249 ft)

P

Lafayette
Campground

R

Lonesome
Lake

N

P R

4,000 FEET

to Mt. Liberty
(4,460 ft)

R P

Mt. Pamigewasset
(2,554 ft) ▲

Visitor Center ■
Restrooms ■

R

Picnic area
Parking
Restrooms
Boat ramp
Hiking trail

I-93 is now the only road through the Notch. To drive from Park Headquarters to the campground or the Flume Visitor Center, you must get on the Interstate.

Plants: Trees of the valley floor are mostly northern hardwoods (uncut since the late 1800s): yellow birch, beech, and sugar maple. Above 2,000 ft. on the hillsides, the less-accessible, never-logged areas, are mature red spruce and balsam fir with some white birch. Flowers of the valley include Dutchman's-breeches, spring beauty, violets, trilliums, and Solomon's-seal. On slopes up to 4,500-ft. of elevation are subalpine flowers, many blooming in May and early June. Above the timberline, some arctic species are found.

Birds: Large flocks of Canada and snow geese often migrate through the valley and bring along with them scores of birdwatchers. Many hawks pass through, as well as golden and bald eagles. About 100 species have been known to use this facility and call it home.

Mammals: Severe winters and snows limit mammal populations. Bear and moose are occasional visitors. Deer are present, though not abundant. More common species include red fox, weasel, snowshoe hare, porcupine, mink, fisher, raccoon, bobcat, chipmunk, mole, and woodchuck. Most streams are too rapid for beaver.

Activities/Facilities: 98 camping sites, hiking, and backpacking (the Appalachian Trail does cross the Park). Several Appalachian Mountain Club huts are within hiking range.

The Flume is a unique geological area with an 800-ft. gorge, walls 70 to 90 ft. high, and width as narrow as 12 ft. Other features include: Avalanche Falls, Liberty Gorge and Cascade, water-washed Table Rock, and glacier-deposited boulders. The area has a network of trails.

Old Man of the Mountains, a 40-ft. profile in granite at 1,200 ft., is located just above Profile Lake.

Cannon Mountain, a popular ski area, is the home of North America's first aerial passenger tram, which transports summer visitors to the top for fine vistas. Adventurous hikers can also hike to the top of the mountain. Bring an ample supply of water.

The Basin, beside the highway, is a 20-ft. granite pothole at the base of a waterfall.

Brook trout are stocked in Echo and Profile Lakes. Swimming is permitted in Echo Lake. Skiing and ski touring are both popular. Cannon Mountain has 26 miles of trails and slopes.

For further information contact: Park Headquarters, Franconia, NH 03580. ☎ (603) 823-5563.

Gap Mountain

Location: From Troy, take SR 12 a ½ mile south. Turn left on Quarry Rd. At the next left, a wooded road continues straight. Watch for trail markers on left.

Just southwest of the more imposing Mt. Monadnock, Gap Mountain has three main peaks, the highest of which is 1,862 ft. The northern and middle peaks are open. The wooded southern peak is a protected natural area. The site includes two bogs and a rich variety of flora and fauna. The Metacomet-Mondadnock Trail crosses the site.

For further information contact: Society for the Protection of New Hampshire Forests, 54 Portsmouth St., Concord, NH 03301. ☎ (603) 224-9945.

Gile Memorial State Forest

Location: NW of Concord: I-89 to Exit 12A then N to SR 4A. Crosses the forest.

The terrain is flat to rolling, with a few hills and scattered small wetlands. The land, once cleared, is now heavily forested with mixed northern hardwoods, pine, and hemlock. Except during the popular hunting seasons, the site has few visitors.

For further information contact: Forest Headquarters, 105 Loudon Rd., Concord, NH 03301. ☎ (603) 271-2214.

Hemenway State Forest

From Conway, 9 miles southwest on SR 16 to Chocorua; the west 2 miles on SR 113, and finally northwest on SR 113A.

Hemenway State Forest, just a little south of the White Mountain National Forest, is rolling to hilly, mostly in conifers, chiefly white pine. The Big Pines Natural Area, 125 acres, is a 150-year-old coniferous forest on a wild river.

Hiking is by far the most popular activity here. Old woods roads and local trails are favorites. Nearby, off SR 16, are trails to Mt. Chocorua and other destinations. (Mt. Chocorua has been called the State's most climbed mountain, but the most popular hiking routes are from the Kancamagus Highway on the north.)

For further information contact: New Hampshire Division of Forests and Lands, 105 Loudon Rd., Concord, NH 03301. ☎ (603) 271-2214.

Lake Francis State Park

Location: From Pittsburg, about 6 miles on US 3, then south to entrance.

This is a small campground built on a 2,051-acre lake in incredible country at the gateway to the Connecticut Lakes. The lake is artificial, supplying water for hydropower. The shore is heavily forested and undeveloped. Unfortunately, there are no hiking trails nearby.

Activities/Facilities: 36 camping sites, boat ramp. Note that fishing is strictly prohibitied.

For further information contact: Division of Parks and Recreation, PO Box 856D, Concord, NH 03301. ☎ (603) 271-3254.

Miller State Park

Location: On SR 101, just 3 miles west of Peterborough.

New Hampshire's oldest park sits atop South Pack Monadnock Mountain. A paved road ascends to the 2,288-ft. summit. Most visitors come to take in the view or to picnic and relax.

Hiking: The Wapack Trail is a 21-mile trail extending from Pack Monadnock Mountain south into Ashburn, MA.

For further information contact: NH Division of Parks & Recreation, 105 Loudon Rd., Concord, NH 03301. ☎ (603) 271-3254.

Moose Brook State Park

Location: Just off US 2, 2 miles west of Gorham.

This is a good base for sightseeing, hiking, and fishing. The Park, at the foot of the Crescent Range, lies near two portions of the White Mountain National Forest. The Presidential Range is south. Moose Brook, a trout stream, is a tributary to the Androscoggin River.

Camping: Forty-two campsites are available.

For further information contact: Park Headquarters, RFD 1, Berlin, NH 03570. ☎ (603) 466-3860.

Mt. Cardigan State Park & State Forest

Location: Off US 4 and SR 118 east of Lebanon.

Mt. Cardigan, at 3,121 ft., is immensely popular with hikers of all ages. A network of trails surrounds the mountain, offering several routes to the top.

Hiking: The shortest and easiest route to the summit is West Ridge Trail, 1.3 miles high. Trails lead to nearby peaks including Firescrew, 3,040 ft., and South, 2,920 ft. There are more than 30 miles of trails in the network.

For further information contact: Division of Parks and Recreation, PO Box 856D, Concord, NH 03301. ☎ (603) 272-3254.

Mt. Kearsarge

Location: From I-89, exit 8; SR 103 to Warner, then due north.

Mt. Kearsarge is a conglomeration of sites, including Roffins and Winslow State Parks, a State Forest, and fish and game lands. At 2,937 ft., it's the highest point for some miles around and provides fine vistas. The top is bare rock showing glacial striations. Upper slopes have stunted, wind-torn spruce. Lower are mixed conifers and northern hardwoods.

For further information contact: Society for the Protection of NH Forests, 54 Portsmouth St., Concord, NH 03301. ☎ (603) 224-9945.

Mt. Monadnock

Location: Off SR 124, about 4 miles north of Jaffrey.

A monadnock is literally an isolated rock mound rising from a plain. The 3,165-ft. peak rises less than 2,000 ft. from its base. Thousands of hikers and nature lovers come on summer and fall weekends to enjoy and hike Mt. Monadnock. An old toll road is now a hikers' route. At one time there were about 80 trails to the summit. Most of them are now closed and revegetating. Of the presently open routes, about a dozen are maintained.

The history of the original forest area is a sad one. After logging came sheep grazing. What forest remained at that time was burned, according to local legend, to drive off wolves. By 1820, the upper 300 to 500 ft. were stripped of soil. The top is now bare rock. On the lower slopes, a regenerated forest is a healthy mix of conifers and hardwoods.

The townspeople of Jaffrey led the preservation movement, buying some of the land in 1884. State acquisition began in 1905. In 1913, the Society for Protection of New Hampshire Forests began purchases. Most of the mountain and lower slopes are now owned by the society and leased to the State. Monadnock State Park now occupies 1,009 acres.

Activites/Facilities: 21 camp sites and 30 miles of challenging hiking trails.

For further information contact: Monadnock State Park, Jaffrey Center, NH 03454. ☎ (603) 532-8862.

Mt. Sunapee State Park

Location: On SR 103, near Newbury.

Mt. Sunapee, 2,720 ft., was quickly being stripped of trees when the Society for the Protection of New Hampshire Forests bought its first 600 acres in 1911, including a 256-acre remnant of virgin timber and Lake Solitude, a small glacial lake.

Mt. Sunapee State Park is a popular place. During winter it's a ski area attracting skiers from all over the New England area. In summer the main chair lift takes visitors to the top, where the lodge offers meals and views. Across the road is Sunapee State Beach, with bathhouse, refreshment stand, picnic area, and launching ramp on 4,085-acre Sunapee Lake.

Challenging hiking trails here – notably the 51-mile Monadnock-Sunapee Greenway that links Mt. Sunapee and Mt. Monadnock.

Camping is available at Pillsbury State Park (see entry).

For further information contact: Division of Parks and Recreation, PO Box 856D, Concord, NH 03301. ☎ (603) 271-3254.

Mt. Washington

Location: From SR 16 north of Pinkham Notch.

The highest peak in the Northeast at 6,288 ft., Mount Washington is one of 11 in the Presidential Range; six of the others tower over 5,000 ft. The mountain is broad and massive, with three major ridges, secondary ridges, numerous valleys and ravines. Slopes range from gentle to steep. Ascending the slopes, many streams rush over falls and cataracts.

Features

The summit has visitor information, rest rooms, post office, snack shop, souvenir shop, and shelter from high winds.

Great Gulf and Tuckerman Ravine are large glacial cirques: dramatic features attractive to hikers and mountain skiers.

Alpine Garden, a natural feature noted for its wildflowers, is on a trail between the auto road and Tuckerman Ravine.

Glen Ellis Falls is one of several impressive falls and cataracts.

Activities and Facilities

Several hiking and backpacking trails cover the mountain. The Appalachian Trail crosses the mountain. Trails link with the trail network of the National Forest. Take extreme caution when attempting any hikes here. There is always danger. The climb is steep and strenuous: about 4,000 ft. in four miles. Winds of 100-mph can occur in any season, along with rain, snow, or cold to threaten hypothermia. Weather, including clouds and fog, can blind the hiker, and can be a grave threat above the timberline where the trails are marked only by stone cairns.

For further information contact: White Mountain National Forest, P.O. Box 638, Laconia, NH 03247. ☎ (603) 524-6450.

Odiorne Point State Park

Location: On SR 1A, just south of Portsmouth.

This fragment of undeveloped seaside and tidal marsh is a war relic. After Pearl Harbor, the Army commandeered the site and evicted residents to install coastal defenses. It became a park in 1961. It has both sandy and rock shores, with stands of scotch pine, oak, and wild rose thickets.

For further information contact: Division of Parks and Recreation, PO Box 856D, Concord, NH 03301. ☎ (603) 271-3254.

Ossipee Lake/Heath Pond Bog

Located: Near the junctions of Routes 16 and 25 in Center Ossipee.

Heath Pond Bog is a National Natural Landmark, a wild area, fragile, undeveloped, and little-publicized. A floating mat of peat covered with sphagnum moss supports a unique plant community, including insectivorous plants, orchids, and heaths. Trees around the pond are chiefly spruce and tamarack. Visitors are asked to stay on the trail.

Fishing: Salmon, lake and brook trout, pickerel, smallmouth bass, cusk, yellow perch, suckers, hornpout, and smelt.
Boating: Launch site on the east shore.

For further information contact: Division of Parks and Recreation, P.0. Box 856D, Concord, NH 03301. ☎ (603) 271-3254.

Pawtuckaway State Park

Location: Route 101 to Route 156 to Raymond.

In summer the 900-ft. beach, 25-acre picnic ground, camping areas, and boating facilities attract crowds from nearby population centers. However, almost 5,000 park acres are undeveloped, and hikers can find quiet trails. To the west are the Pawtuckaway Mountains: the highest is 1,011-ft. North Peak. Incredible views are seen from the fire tower on South Peak. A stream flows through a hemlock ravine.

Activities/Facilities: 170 campsites, fishing for small- and large-mouth bass, and several boating ramps.

For further information contact: Pawtuckaway State Park, Raymond, NH 03077. ☎ (603) 895-3031.

Peabody Forest

Location: From Gorham, 3½ miles east on US 2.

The trail passes among large, breathtaking white pines and hemlocks in the south, then stately northern hardwoods. The Peabody Trail continues beyond the site along Peabody Brook toward Giant Falls and the Mahoosuc Range.

For further information contact; NH Division of Parks & Recreation, 105 Loudon Rd., Concord, NH 03301. ☎ (603) 271-3254.

Pillsbury State Park

Location: On SR 31, 3½ miles N of Washington.

The last of several sawmill owners here was one of the founders of the Society for the Protection of New Hampshire Forests. In 1920 he deeded 2,400 acres to the State as a forest reservation. In the 1930s, the Civilian Conservation Corps (CCC) restored ponds once choked with sawdust and rebuilt dams. The site was opened as a State Park in 1952. Only 151 acres have been developed; the rest remains a near-wilderness. Recently, a corridor has been acquired, linking Pillsbury with Mount Sunapee State Park (see entry).

Activities/Facilities: 20 primitive sites on 150-acre May Pond, 20 miles of hiking trails. The 51-mile Monadnock-Sunapee Greenway crosses the Park.
Fishing: Largemouth bass, pickerel, hornpout, and yellow perch.
Canoeing: Only hand-carried crafts may be used.

For further information contact : Division of Parks and Recreation, PO Box 856D, Concord, NH 03301. ☎ (603) 271-3254.

Pine River State Forest

Location: Connects Pine River Pond with Ossipee Lake, crossing SR 16.

Pine River is canoe-navigable for 20 miles, but of course subject to changes in the weather. Use common sense when deciding to canoe this river. Class II rapids are in the five miles from Pine River Pond to Granite Road. From there the river flows gently through unspoiled forest, with stretches of sandy bottom, and deep pools. Wildflowers abound in season. Some canoeists camp along the way. It's a "best kept secret" stream, with good fishing.

For further information contact: Pine River State Forest, 105 Loudon Rd., Concord, NH 03301. ☎ (603) 271-2214.

Pisgah State Park

Location: Just off of SR 63, outside of Chesterfield.

A 20-square-mile wilderness in fast-growing southern New Hampshire may seem improbable, but a management plan adopted in 1987 by the State's park, forest, and wildlife agencies would maintain Pisgah as a place "where visitors can experience a sense of relative solitude and remoteness from civilization."

This area was called "the Pisgah wilderness" before the State purchased it. Terrain is mostly a series of low ridges dividing valleys that have streams, ponds, and marshes. The highest point is 1,416-ft. Davis Hill. Mt. Pisgah is 1,303 ft., and Pisgah Pond, the largest water body, is about 1½ miles long; Fullam Pond is about half that length.

Birds: Waterfowl, herons, many hawks, and owls. Fall roosting of grackles at Fullam Pond. Many warblers in season.
Mammals: Include beaver, bobcat, fisher, coyote, red fox, porcupine, raccoon, and deer.
Activities/Facilities: Hiking (30 miles of old logging roads), nature study, cross-country skiing, picnicking, fishing (trout and bass), hunting (deer and grouse), non-motorized boating, and berry picking.

For further information contact: Division of Parks and Recreation, PO Box 856D, Concord, NH 03301. ☎ (603) 271-3254.

Squam Lakes Region

Location: From Route 93, Exit 24 just outside of Holderness.

Squam Lake, 6,765 acres, a popular fishing and summer home location, is a natural water body whose level was raised by a dam. It has a 61-mile rocky, wooded shoreline. Linked to it by a narrow waterway is 408-acre Little Squam Lake. If things look familiar when you first arrive, you may recognize it from the movie "On Golden Pond" that was filmed here.

The Squam Lakes Association was originally organized in 1905, with the primary mission of protecting the lake's water quality. Its current publication demands that residents and visitors alike keep soap, detergent, and human waste out of the lake, use fertilizer sparingly, have septic tanks pumped every three years, and not use lumber treated with creosote or pentachlorophenol for docks or decks.

The Squam Lakes Association maintains three primitive lakeside campsites, two of which require boat access. Reservations are required and often difficult to come by.

More than 40 miles of trails extend north into the Squam Mountains and beyond to the trails of the White Mountain National Forest.

Squam Lake is well known for its salmon and lake trout. Also, smallmouth bass, pickerel, white and yellow perch, hornpout, whitefish, cusk, and smelt.

For further information contact: Squam Lakes Region, PO Box 204, Holderness, NH 03245. ☎ (603) 968-7336.

Wapack National Wildlife Refuge

Location: Accessible via trail from Miller State Park.

This land was acquired by gift, not purchase. On 2,288-ft. North Pack Monadnock Mountain, 1,200 ft. above the valley floor, land is rugged, unspoiled, forested, with bogs and swamps, ledges, cliffs, open alpine, flats and streams. Visitors are few.

Birds: Without a doubt, this is a fabulous place to watch the migration of hawks. Nesting species include tree sparrow, winter wren, Swainson's thrush magnolia warbler, and white-throated sparrow.

Mammals: Include deer, fisher, mink, squirrel porcupine, chipmunk, mice, voles, weasel, raccoon, fox, bobcat, snowshoe hare.

Hiking: The Wapack Trail crosses the site.

For further information contact : Wapack National Wildlife Refuge, c/o Great Meadows National Wildlife Refuge, Weir Hill Rd., Sudbury, MA 01776. ☎ (617) 443-4661.

White Lake State Park

Location: Outside of West Ossipee, ½ mile N on SR 16.

The lake is a just over a half-mile long with a popular, high-quality, natural beach. One of New Hampshire's most popular camping spots, it is very crowded in the swimming season. The site includes some forest, a black spruce bog, and two small bog ponds. It's near Hemenway State Forest (see entry).

Camping: 173 camping sites are available from late May to mid-October.

For further information contact: White Lake State Park, West Ossipee, NH 03890. ☎ (603) 323-7350.

White Mountain National Forest

Location: Crossed by US 2, I-93, US 302, and other routes.
(Covers huge area in north-central NH.)

White Mountain National Forest covers over 10% of New Hampshire's land area – the highest percentage of federal land for any eastern State.

The White Mountains dominate northern New Hampshire and extend well into Maine. Without a doubt, the most striking feature is the Presidential Range, a chain of peaks named for American Presidents, a number of them more than a mile high. Mt. Washington, at 6,288 ft., is highest of all. Along the ridges is an alpine zone about eight miles long and two miles wide, treeless and wind-swept.

Although the Forest produces timber, about 95% of it is natural in appearance, showing no conspicuous signs of human damage. On the average, 3,400 acres are logged each year, only 1,900 acres in obvious openings. The 5% also includes ski areas, campgrounds, roads, and service areas.

Recreational use of the Forest totals about 3,000,000 visitors per year. On days when traffic is heavy at Pinkham, Crawford, and Franconia Notches, motorized sightseeing appears to be the chief visitor activity, but it accounts for only one-fifth of the visitor percentage. Camping and picnicking make up a quarter of the total, downhill skiing about one-twelfth. Almost half of the visitor-days are spent in backcountry hiking, hunting, fishing.

There are 1,167 miles of hiking trails and 100 miles of cross-country ski trails. About half of the Forest is open to winter off-road vehicle travel, chiefly on 300-plus miles of winter ORV (off-road vehicle) trails.

The Forest offers opportunities for extensive backpacking, challenging mountain hikes, and even easy day walks in scenic valleys. The hiking season in the mountains is generally from June to mid-October, but weather on the mountains can be severe in any season – windier, colder, and wetter than in the valleys. Above timberline where trails are marked by stone cairns, many hikers have lost their way and some, their lives. Proper clothing and gear, and knowing what to do in case of trouble, are essential to full enjoyment of these lofty places.

Great cirques in the mountainsides mark the action of past glaciers. Rivers have cut down through faults, forming steep-sided ravines, here called "notches," of which Franconia Notch and Crawford Notch are best known.

Throughout the Forest are incredible waterfalls, cascades, pools, ponds, vistas, and other natural attractions, as follows:

Presidential Range/Dry River Wilderness – 27,380 acres, includes the 4,930-acre Alpine Area, treeless along the ridge tops, with many alpine plants. Wildflowers blooming in the brief summer include: alpine azalea, bearberry, bluet, goldenrod, speedwell, black crowberry, bluebell, dwarf cinquefoil, dwarf willow, eyebright, Labrador tea, Lapland rose bay, mountain cranberry, and pale laurel.

Great Gulf Wilderness – 5,552 acres, on the north slope of Mt. Washington adjoining the Alpine Area. The largest cirque in the White Mountains walls, rising up to 1,600 ft., with old-growth red spruce and balsam fir. Many trails.

Pemigewasset Wilderness – 45,000 acres, between Franconia Notch and Crawford Notch. Mountainous, forested, bounded by the Appalachian Trail; also internal trails.

Pemigewasset Extension – 16,000 acres, bordering the east side of the Pemigewasset Wilderness. Steep, heavily forested, no trails.

Sandwich Range Wilderness – 25,000 acres, between the Kancamagus Highway, SR 112 and the southern boundary of the Forest. It includes the Bowl Natural Area, which has a virgin climax spruce/fir forest and virgin climax northern hardwood forest within a large cirque.

Pinkham Notch Scenic Area – a cluster of features on both sides of SR 16, with Mt. Washington on the west, Wildcat Mountain on the east, Tuckerman and Huntington ravines, Alpine Gardens, Crystal Cascades, Glen Ellis Falls.

Rocky Gorge Scenic Area – on the Kancamagus Highway. A narrow gorge cut by the Swift River bordering tall red spruce.

Scenic drives include:
- Kancamagus Highway between Lincoln and Conway.
- Lower Falls, Greeley Ponds and Rocky Gorge Scenic Areas, Sabbaday Falls, campgrounds, and trailheads.
- Jefferson Notch Road, north from Crawford Notch. Highest road in the state, narrow and steep. Careful!
- Evans Notch, from Chatham north on SR 113 into Maine. The Maine-portion of the Forest is the Evans Notch Ranger District.

Aerial tramways are on Cannon, Black, Wildcat, and Loon mountains.

Birds: Species common in summer include great blue herons, mallards, black ducks, wood ducks, rock and mourning doves, black-billed cuckoos, chimney swifts, house sparrow, bobolink, eastern meadowlark, red-winged black-bird, common grackle, brown-headed cowbird, scarlet tanager, rose-breasted grosbeak, purple finch, American goldfinch, ruby-throated hummingbirds, belted kingfishers, northern flickers, yellow-bellied sapsuckers, hairy and downy woodpeckers, eastern kingbirds, eastern phoebes, yellow-bellied and least flycatchers, eastern wood-pewees; blue jays, common ravens, American crows, black-capped and boreal chickadees, white-breasted and red-breasted nuthatches, brown creepers, winter wrens, gray catbirds, cedar waxwings, European starlings, brown thrashers, American robins; wood, hermit, Swainson's, and gray-cheeked thrushes; golden-crowned and ruby-crowned kinglets; solitary and red-eyed vireos. Warblers: black-and-white, Nashville, parula, magnolia, blue, yellow-rumped, black-throated, green, blackburnian, chestnut-sided, and blackpoll, ovenbird, northern, waterthrush, yellowthroat, Canada, American redstart. Sparrows: savannah, chipping, white-throated, song. Slate-colored junco; tree, bank, and barn swallows.

Mammals: The Forest has over 750 moose and they are seen more often than deer. Other common species include moles, shrews, bats, snowshoe hare, black bear, raccoon, woodchuck, chipmunk, red and flying squirrels, red fox, skunk, porcupine, beaver, muskrat fisher, otter, and bobcat. Uncommon: lynx, pine marten.

Facilities/Activites: 22 campgrounds with 844 sites. Campgrounds usually open May 15 through October 15. Several are open in winter but roads aren't plowed. Most campgrounds are filled during summer and fall peaks. Note: absolutely no reservations are accepted.

Nature trails: Begin at the Russell Colbath Historic Site and near the Covered Bridge campground on the Kancamagus Highway. With over 1,000 miles of trails to choose among, it's advisable to study one of the hiking guides before setting forth. Trailside facilities include 43 shelters, eight Appalachian Mountain Club huts, and eight cabins.

Hunting: Very popular for deer, bear, raccoon, rabbit, ruffed grouse, woodcock, and duck.

Fishing: Saco and Swift rivers and their tributaries. The Pemigewasset, once heavily polluted, now has good fishing.

Skiing: Areas are located on the Forest land. Tuckerman Ravine has been called "the only true alpine ski area east of the Rockies." Cross-country skiing opportunities are unlimited, with several hundred miles of marked trails for skiing and snowshoeing.

For further information contact: Forest Headquarters, 719 Main St., Laconia, NH 03247. ☎ (603) 524-6450.

Rhode Island

State Parks

Beavertail State Park

Directions from Providence: Take Interstate Route 95 South to Route 4 South to Route 1 South. Then take Route 138 East to North Main Road. This connects with Southeast Ave. which will take you to Beavertail Road.

Activities: Fishing, hiking, picnicking and scenic overlooks.
Facilities: Portable restrooms – year round; public phone and information – seasonal; paved parking lots.

For further information contact: Superintendent of Beavertail State Park, c/o Goddard Memorial State Park, Ives Road, Warwick, RI 02818.

Blackstone River Valley

Location: Near Route 122 in Uxbridge, MA.

The Blackstone River Valley National Heritage is a special type of park. It is a region of 250,000 acres between Worcester, Massachusetts, and Providence, Rhode Island. The National Heritage Corridor included whole cities and towns, dozens of villages, and 500,000 people. The Federal Government does not own or manage the land as it does in more traditional National Parks. Instead, people, businesses, non-profit historic and environmental organizations, 20 local and two state governments, the National Park Service, and a unifying commission work together to protect its special identity and prepare for the valley's future.

The Blackstone River Valley illustrates a major revolution in America's past: the Age of Industry. The way people lived during this turning point in history can still be seen in the valley's villages, farms, cities, and riverways – in the working landscape. In 1790 American craftsmen built the first machines that successfully used waterpower to spin cotton. American's first factory, Slater Mill, was built on the banks of the Blackstone River. Here, industrial America was born. This revolutionary way of using waterpower spread quickly throughout the valley and New England. It changed nearly everything. The story of the American Industrial Revolution can still be seen and told 200 years later in the Blackstone River Valley. Thousands of structures and whole landscapes show the radical changes in the way people lived and worked. Native Americans, European colonizers, farmers, craftsmen, industrialists, and continuing waves of immigrants all left the imprint of their work on the land. The farms, a hilltop market center, mill villages, cities, dams, canals, roads, and railroads are all cultural products of tremendous social and economic power. These features show how the force of technology and invention, labor and management, commerce and government, and pollution and recovery affect us today.

Visitors should stop at the Slate Mill Historical Site in Pawtucket Rhode Island to pick up additional information on places to visit in the National Heritage Corridor. Visitors can walk along sections of the Blackstone Canal and Towpath at the state parks in Lincoln, Rhode Island and Uxbridge, Massachusetts.

For more information please contact: Visitor's Center, 414 Massasoit Rd., Worcester, MA. ☎ (508) 754-7363.

Brenton Point State Park

Directions from Providence: Take Interstate Route 195 East to Route 136 South. Follow Route 114 South (West Main Road) to Route 138 South on to Broadway. This leads to Downtown Newport. Follow signs to Ocean Drive.

Activities: Fishing, hiking, picnicking, and scenic overlooks.

Facilities: Restrooms, information, 30 picnic tables, public phone, concession stand, public gardens, and paved parking lot. Fishing and boat ramp at King's Beach located down the road from Brenton State Park. Accessible year round, weather permitting.

For further information contact: Superintendent, Brenton Point State Park, Ocean Drive, Newport, RI 02840. ☎ (401) 847-2400 (Fort Adams State Park).

Burlingame State Park

*Directions from Providence: Take I-95 south
to Route 4 south onto Route 1 south to Charlestown.
Turn at Burlingame Campground sign.*

Activities: Camping, fishing, swimming, picnicking, boating, hiking, snowmobiling, recreation programs and summer concerts. Lifeguards on duty 10 am to 6 pm. Activities offered during season only.

Facilities: 755 campsites, restrooms, coin-operated hot showers, water, public phones, recreation center, camp store, hiking trails, and boat ramp. Facilities for the handicapped. Water available throughout the campground.

Fees
Tent and recreational vehicle sites (no hookups)
Residents: $8 per night
Non-residents: $12 per night
Visitors: $2 per car
Second car pass: $2 per car - resident
Second car pass: $3 per car - non-resident

Available on a first-come, first-served basis only. No reservations.

For further information contact: Superintendent, Burlingame State Park, Route 1, Charlestown, RI 02813. ☎ (401) 322-7337 (seasonal); ☎ (401) 322-7994 (seasonal); ☎ (401) 322-8910 (year round).

Charlestown Breachway State Park

Directions: From 95 North, take Exit 92 to Route 2 East. Follow Route 2 East to Route 78 East. At the light at Route 78 andRoute 1, turn left to Route 1. Follow 8 miles to the Charlestown Breachway Exit off Route 1 (Exit just pass Bess Eaton Donuts). At the next intersection go straight, then left at the stop sign, then right onto Charlestown Beach Road. Follow to end
Park is at the end of the road.

Activities: Swimming, saltwater beach with lifeguards (in season), fishing, boating, boat ramp with access to coastal ponds, camping for 75 self-contained motorhomes and trailers only. No tents or tent trailers.

Fees:

> *Day Parking*
> RI Residents: $8
> Non-Residents: $10
> *Parking Season Pass*
> RI Residents: $25
> Non-Residents: $50
> *Camping*
> RI Residents: $8
> Out of State: $12
> *Extra Vehicle (1 only)*
> RI Residents: $2

Seven day maximum stay with a four-day break between stays (mid June to Labor Day).

For further information contact: Division of Parks & Recreation, 22 Hayes St., Providence RI, 02908. ☎ (401) 277-2632. Or ☎ (401) 364-7000 (4/15 to 10/31); ☎ (401) 322-8910 (off-season only).

Colt State Park

Directions from Providence: Take Interstate Route 195 East to Route 114 south to Hope Street in Bristol.

Samuel Colt, chairman of the board of the United States Rubber Company, created an extraordinary farm. He bought and combined three farms and designed a system of roads that linked them together as one. The stone bridge that still spans the Mill Gut was part of this road system. His large summer house, the Casino, was constructed on the shore of Narragansett Bay. Two smaller guest houses were also built near the water. Closer to the stone barn was a farmhouse where some of his farm employees lived. Bronze statues of horses, deer, and Greek gods and goddesses looked out over the meadows where Colonel Colt's prize Jersey herd grazed.

Colt Park's 460 acres slope gently down to the Mill Gut Salt Marsh and to Narragansett Bay. Within the park are freshwater streams, a large salt marsh, oak and maple woods, as well as many acres of fields. Stone walls that criss-cross these fields are evidence that the park was once farmland. Large ornamental trees, once planted by Colonel Colt in the early 1900s, now provide a shady picnic grove near the shore. Looking out over Narragansett Bay, one can see the north end of Prudence Island, another part of the Rhode Island state park system. A passenger ferry now runs from Colt Park to the Island.

Activities: Passenger ferry from Colt Park to the north end of Prudence Island, naturalist programs, picnicking, hiking, snowmobiling, jogging, summer concerts, fishing, boating, and bicycling. Weddings and other ceremonies in Chapel-By-The-Sea.
Facilities: Office and information, restrooms (seasonal), ceremonial area, 16 fireplaces (reservation required), 300 picnic tables, bridle paths (two miles), open fields, bike path (3.2 miles), water bubblers, jogging trails with warm-up station, gazebo with two charcoal grills and eight picnic tables.

Fees:
  Entrance fees seven days per week, May 1 to September 30
  Residents: $2 per car
  Non-residents: $4 per car
  Special sites
  Gazebo: $35 per day
  Fireplace sites: $10 to $35 daily (depending on site)
  Ceremonial areas: $15 for three hours and $30 per day
  Season Passes - beaches and parks
  Residents: $25
  Non-residents: $50
  Resident seniors: $12.50
  Non-resident seniors: $25
  RI residents: park pass only – $10
  Ferry round-trip rates
  Adults 18 and over: $5
  Children 6 to 17: $2.50
  Children under 6: free
  Charters attending naturalist program on Prudence Island:
    $1.50 per person

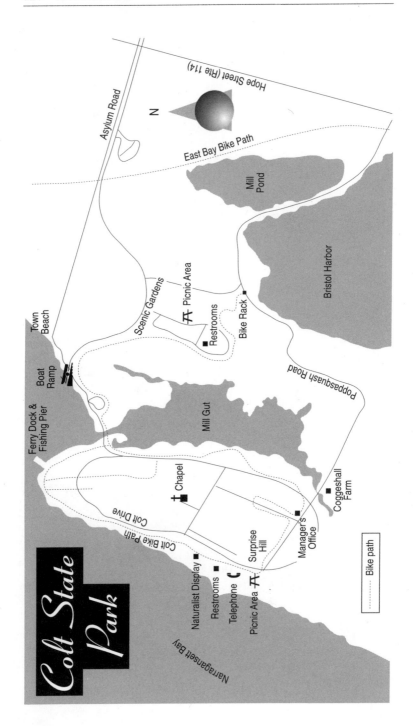

For further information contact: Superintendent, Colt State Park, Route 114 (Hope Street), Bristol, RI 02809. ☎ (401) 253-7482 (year round); Fax (401) 253-6766.

East Bay Bike Path

Directions from Providence: Easy access from Colt State Park or Haines State Park. Can be accessed from any of 49 intersections from Providence to Bristol.

This is the first bicycle facility undertaken by the state of Rhode Island. Upon completion, the path will run from Providence to Independence Park in Bristol, with a total length of 14½ miles.

The path was created to encourage an alternative mode of transportation and an appreciation of the natural beauty found in the state. You may observe a variety of animal and plant life.

The East Bay Bicycle Path intersects 49 streets, so please use caution. There are two traffic signal intersections, at County Road in Barrington and Main Street (Route 114) in Warren.

Mileage:
- Phase 1 – Riverside Square to Barrington County Road – 4.17 miles
- Phase 2 – Barrington County Road to Franklin Street, Warren – 2.38 miles
- Phase 3 – Franklin Street, Warren to Independence Park, Bristol – 3.87 miles
- Phase 4 – Riverside Square to India Point Park, Providence – 3.98 miles

Activities: Bicycling, 14½ miles.
Facilities: 10-foot-wide paved path with two-foot grass shoulders and center lines for separate lanes. Path passes through Colt, Hains, and Squantum Woods State Parks. Refer to those areas for additional facilities.

For further information contact: Colt State Park, Division of Parks & Recreation, 22 Hayes St. Providence, RI 02908. ☎ (401) 253-7482.

Fisherman's Memorial State Park

From Providence: Take Interstate Route 95 south to Route 4,
south to Route 1, south to Route 108, to Narrangansett, RI.

Activities: Tent and recreational vehicle camping, recreational programs, and summer concerts (all seasons, check with permit office for schedules).

Facilities: 182 campsites, 40 with water, electric and sewer, 107 with water and electric, and 35 with no hookups. All with tables and fireplaces. Three restrooms, all with coin-operated hot showers. Wood and ice available. Recreational field, two tennis courts, two basketball courts, one horseshoe court, and playground equipment available. Observation area, permit office, and information. Facilities for the handicapped.

Fees:

Area 1, electric, water and sewer
$12 per night, RI residents
$16 per night, non-residents
Area 2 and 4, electric and water
$10 per night, RI residents
$14 per night, non-residents
Area 3, no hook-ups
$8 per night, RI residents
$12 per night, non-residents
Visitors - $2 per car
Second car pass - $2 residents, $3 non-residents

Reservations: Send self-addressed stamped envelope to Fishermen's Memorial State Park for reservation forms and any additional information.

Fishermen's Memorial State Park
DEM Division of Parks and Recreation
2321 Hartford Ave.
Johnston, RI 02919
☎ (401) 277-2632.

Reservation requests should be sent directly to: Fishermen's Memorial State Park, 1011 Pt. Judith Road, Narragansett, RI 02882-5598. Reservations will be accepted by mail only and must be postmarked no earlier than midnight on 14th of January annually.

Fort Adams State Park

From Providence: Take I-95 south to Route 4, South to Route 138 to Jamestown. Keep on Route 138 to Newport Bridge. Right after bridge take DOWNTOWN EXIT and follow signs to Fort Adams State Park (Newport Bridge Toll: Token or $2 each way).

Activities

Swimming: Lifeguard on duty, 10 am to 6 pm weekends and holidays from Memorial Day to 3rd weekend in June, then daily until Labor Day.

Fishing/Boating: Sail and power boating, windsurfing, soccer, rugby (by permits only), picnicking, summer concerts and festivals, roadraces, scenic overlook, and special events.

Sail Newport: A non-profit community sailing facility offering sailboat instruction, rental, drysail storage areas, and hoist operation. Handicap sailing available. Sail Newport also organizes regattas and other sailing events. For more information ☎ (401) 846-1983 year round.

The Museum of Yachting: Displays center around "Yachting in Newport – the Golden Age," a show of photography, models, costumes, boats and yachting memorabilia from the turn of the century. Open daily from second weekend of May to November 1st. Other months by appointment. Entrance fees: $2 per adult, $1 for Senior Citizens, free to children under 12. For more information, ☎ (401) 847-1018.

Eisenhower House: Conference & Seminar Center overlooking Narragansett Bay. Also available for social events. For more information, ☎ (401) 847-6740 or (401) 277-6790.

Facilities

Bathing beach, boat ramps, fishing piers, sailing center, picnic areas with 35 picnic tables and 10 fireplaces, concession stands, restrooms, water bubblers, two soccer fields, one rugby field (by permit only), overnight parking for cars only, information center, and public phones. All Seasonal – launch services from/to downtown and moored boats. Open year round from sunrise to sunset.

Fees:

Entrance - 7:30 am to 4 pm, Memorial Day to September 30th
$2 per car: residents
$4 per car: non-residents
Season Passes:
$10 per car: PARKS ONLY (residents)
$5 per car: RI senior citizens
Parks & Beach Pass:
$25 per car: residents
$12.50 per car: senior residents
$50 per car: non-residents
$25 senior: non-residents

Soccer & Rugby Field Rental:

$25 per 2 hours: ages 17 and over
$35 for 10 games maximum: youth under 17
$5 per game over 10 games

Mule Barn Rental:

$200 per day: entire building
$ 50 per day: showers and lockers only

Overnight parking:

For cars only: no camping
$3 per night per car: RI residents
$6 per night per car: non-residents
Season permits: available for cars only
$35 per car: RI residents
$70 per car: non-residents

For more information contact: Fort Adams State Park, Newport, RI 42840. ☎ (401) 847-2400.

Fort Wetherill State Park

From Providence: Take Interstate Route 95 South to Route 4. Follow to Route 1 South, then Route 138 East to Canonicus Ave. From here onto Walcott Ave. then to Fort Wetherill Road.

Activities: Picnicking, boating, scuba diving, saltwater fishing, and scenic overlooks.
Facilities: 25 picnic tables, boat ramp, restrooms (seasonal), two portable toilets at scuba area and boat ramp (year round), paved parking lots with scenic overlooks, public phone, office, and information (seasonal).

For further information contact: Superintendent, Fort Wetherill Road, Jamestown, RI 02835 (for mailing address see Goddard Memorial State Park). ☎ (401) 423-1771 (seasonal).

Goddard Memorial State Park

From Providence: Take Interstate Route 95 south to East Greenwich Exit. Turn right on Division Street, to Route 1 South. Follow signs to Goddard Memorial State Park.

*L*ittle more than 100 years ago, the shady woodlands along the shore of Greenwich Bay were barren sand dunes. In 1874 the owner of the land, Henry Russell, began a tree-planting project that he continued for 30 years. He began by planting acorns and later raised a wide variety of seedling trees to transplant into the dry sandy soil. After Russell died, Colonel Goddard continued to plant trees for another 20 years. Foresters from the United States Forest Service visited the site in the early 1900s and called this "the finest example of private forestry in America."

In November 1927, this land was given to the State of Rhode Island in memory of Colonel Goddard. Today, people can picnic, ride on horseback, or walk in the shade of huge old trees that had been planted by Russell and Goddard.

Activities: Saltwater bathing (lifeguard on duty 10 am to 6 pm), roadraces, picnicking, golfing, hiking, concerts, fishing, boating, ice skating, and special events. (All seasonal – check with permit office for schedules).

Facilities: Saltwater beach and bathhouse facility, newly renovated nine-hole golf course with pro shop, equestrian show area, 18 miles of bridle trails, two concession stands, water bubblers, 155 fireplaces with picnic tables (reservations required), 200 portable stove areas with picnic tables, 11 game fields (reservations required during season), boat ramp, performing arts center (renovated Carousel Building) for special events, beach picnic shelter, gazebo for large group outings, Information and Permit Building.

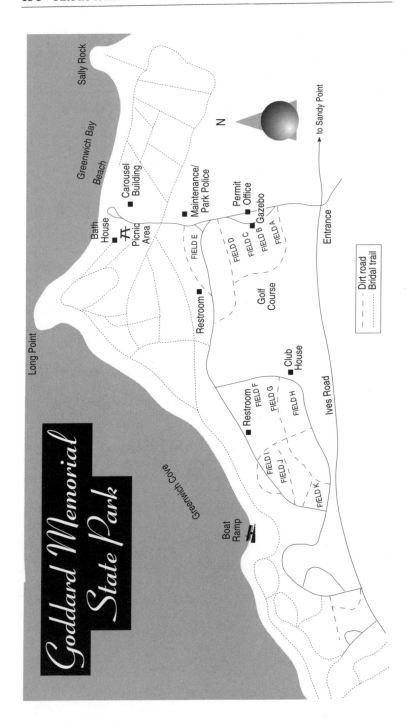

Goddard Memorial State Park

Dirt road
Bridal trail

Operational Times and Information:
Park hours: Open year round - sunrise to sunset
Picnic season (from April 15 to October 31st)
Reservations for groups accepted starting March 15th annually
Call Park Permit office for information on park regulations
Office hours: 8-3:30 (winter), 7:30-6 (summers, weekends, holidays)

Golf - Nine Hole Course
Open Apr. 15 through last Saturday of Nov. (weather permitting)
Regular hours: 8 am to 3:30 pm (winter)
7:30 am to 6 pm (summer)
Weekdays: $6 (nine holes)
Weekends and holidays: $8 (nine holes)
Senior Citizens (65 and older) Weekdays: $3 (nine holes);
weekends and Holidays - $4 (nine holes)
100% Disabled by Social Security Standards (with proper iden-
tification cards) - no charge
Clubhouse ☎ 884-9834 for information

Equestrian show area:
$15 per day
$50 per season with reservations

Entrance fees:
Charged from May 1st through September 30th
Rates per car:
Residents, $2
Non-residents, $4
Park-only passes:
Residents, $10
Senior citizens, $5

Telephone Numbers:
(401) 884-2010 - Year round
(401) 884-9834 - Golf course clubhouse -seasonal
(401) 884-9620 - Beach bathhouse - seasonal
(401) 884-0088 - Ranger headquarters - Seasonal

For further information contact: Superintendent, Ives Road, Warwick, RI 02818.

Haines Memorial State Park

*From Providence: Interstate Route 195 east to Veterans Memorial Parkway
(Riverside Exit) to Route 103 to Metropolitan Park Drive to Haines State Park.*

Activities: Picnicking, boating, softball, hiking, and fishing.
Facilities: 33 picnic sites with fireplaces and tables available on a
first-come, first-served basis, a boat ramp, and a flush toilet facility.

For further information contact: Superintendent, Route 103, East Providence, RI 02915 (for mailing address, see Colt State Park). ☎ (401) 253-7482.

Lincoln Woods State Park

From Providence: Take Interstate Route 95 North to Route 146 north exit for Lincoln Woods State Park - off Route 146 north.

Activities: Freshwater bathing (lifeguards on duty from 9 am to 8 pm seasonal), picnicking, boating (under 10 hp motors allowed), baseball, fishing (freshwater), horseback riding, snowmobiling, ice skating, recreational programs, roadraces and special events (all seasonal, contact park office for schedules). No outboard motors allowed Saturday, Sunday, and holidays during season.

Facilities: 92 picnic tables and fireplace sites (reservations accepted), two game fields, a little league field, two picnic shelters, 10miles of bridle trails, a boat ramp, bathhouse, restrooms and cold showers, concession stand, office, and information. Reservations required for picnic tables and fireplaces during season.

Fees:
>1 table and fireplace: $2
>Game field: $8 per day
>Season rates per team for Little League: $25

Entrance Fees:
>*Weekends and holidays from Memorial Day to June 21*
>$2 per car: RI residents
>$4 per car: non-residents

Season Passes:
>*Starting June 21 to Labor Day (7 days a week) same rates*
>*Parks and beaches:*
>$25 resident; $12.50 seniors
>$50 non-resident; $25 non-resident seniors
>*Parks only:*
>$10 resident; $5 non-resident

For more information write: Great Road, Route 123, Lincoln, RI 02865. ☎ (401) 723-7892.

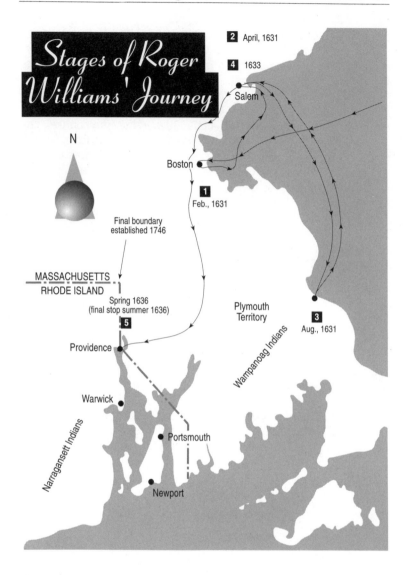

Stages of Roger Williams' Journey

N

2 April, 1631

4 1633

Salem

Boston

1 Feb., 1631

Final boundary
established 1746

MASSACHUSETTS
RHODE ISLAND

Spring 1636
(final stop summer 1636)

5

Providence

Plymouth
Territory

3 Aug., 1631

Wampanoag Indians

Warwick

Narragansett Indians

Portsmouth

Newport

Roger Williams National Memorial

Location: 282 N. Main St., Providence.

Roger Williams National Memorial commemorates the life and
work of the early American statesman and champion of the great
ideas underlying modern democracy. Roger Williams, who lived

from 1603 to 1683, defied the united powers of church and state and demanded for all the right to freedom of conscience. After banishment by Massachusetts Bay Colony in 1635, he found the colony of Rhode Island and Providence Plantations, providing a place for a "lively experiment" in religious liberty. That "no man should be molested for his conscience" – the rule in Rhode Island from the beginning – was a radical, subversive idea in the 17th century. The principle sprang from Williams' passionate search for spiritual truth. This park, located on a common lot of the original settlement of Providence, pays tribute to the "seeker" whose life and thought still holds meaning for society.

Roger Williams National Memorial was authorized in 1965. The land was purchased by the National Park Service in 1974. The park consists of four and a half intensely landscaped acres in downtown Providence. The Visitor Center, at 282 N. Main Street, features exhibits and a slide show.

The Hahn Memorial marks the site of the "spring of fresh water" used by the Williams family, whose house stood across Main Street, then called Towne Streete. Almost the entire village of Providence was destroyed during "King Philip's Ware" in 1676. Since then, any remaining vestige of the village of Providence, as Roger Williams knew it, has been obliterated by the city's growth.

Roger Williams National Monument is administered by the National Park Service, US Department of the Interior. The Superintendent's address is 282 N. Main Street, Providence, RI 02903.

Vermont

State Parks

The following are the Vermont State Parks' regional addresses where reservations can be made from the first Tuesday in January through May 14. After that, contact the park directly.

Region 1(southeast)
Ranger Supervisor
RR1 Box 33
North Springfield, VT 05150
☎ (802) 886-2434

Region II(southwest)
Ranger Supervisor
RR2, Box 2161
Pittsford, VT 05763-9713
☎ (802) 483-2001

Region III (northwest)
Ranger Supervisor
111 West Street
Essex Junction, VT 05452
☎ (802)-879-5674

Region IV(northeast)
Ranger Supervisor
324 North Main Street
Barre, VT 05641
☎ (802) 479-4280

Camping

Rates: Base rates are for up to four people at a single site. Each additional person, age four years and older, will be charged $3 at a tent site and $4 at a lean-to. Maximum of eight people per camping site.

Age: There must be at least one person 18 years of age with each camping party.

Pets: Pets are permitted in camping areas, but may be restricted to certain sites. Proof of rabies vaccination must be presented at check-in. Pets are not permitted in day use areas.

Reservations: Requests must be postmarked no earlier than January 1. All Parks will accept reservation requests for specific sites for four or more consecutive nights. Beginning May 15, most parks will accept requests for fewer than four nights, but may not guarantee a specific site.

Mailed reservations are accepted in order of receipt of completed application with full payment at the appropriate regional office (or park if after May 15). Note: You must include a $3 non-refundable reservation fee.

Ascutney State Park

Location: From I-91, exit 8, north 2 miles on US 5.

This is said to be the first American mountain with a developed hiking trail, and the ancestor of the Long Trail and Appalachian Trail. The mountain is a monadnock, not part of a chain, and is visible for miles around. Its peak is 3,144 ft. in elevation, almost half a mile above its base. Its slopes are generally moderate but are steep in places. At one point water trickles over a steep ledge, forming an impressive ice sheet in winter.

The mountain forest is not pristine. It was severely burned in a summer-long forest fire in 1883, then much of it flattened by a great hurricane in 1938. Its crest is decorated with television, radio, and microwave towers. A motor road goes almost to the top, a trail the rest of the way. It's a splendid view from there. The area has good hiking trails.

Camping: 49 sites, including lean-tos.

Hiking/Backpacking: Trailside camping is permitted. Three trails go to the summit. Two can be combined in a seven-mile circle hike.
Hunting: Deer, wild turkey, and grouse.
Ski touring: On scenic road when unplowed.

For more information contact: Ascutney State Park, RR1 Box 33, North Springfield, VT 05150. ☎ (802) 886-2434.

Atherton Meadow Wildlife Management Area

Location: Near the Massachusetts border, west of Whitingham on SR 100.

This area has no frontage on the reservoir, but there is public access at the north end and the fishing is good. The reservoir covers 2,157 acres and is about eight miles long.

Birds: Includes eastern bluebirds, black-capped chickadees, brown creepers, goldfinches, purple finches, ruffed grouse, flycatchers, kinglets, vireos, cedar waxwings, American woodcocks, wood-peckers, various wood warblers.
Mammals: Includes deer, snowshoe hare, red and gray squirrels, chipmunk, red and gray foxes, coyote, black bear, bobcat, raccoon, otter, mink, weasel, fisher, beaver.

For further information contact : District Wildlife Biologist, RR #1, Box 33, North Springfield, VT 05150. ☎ (802) 886-2215.

Bomoseen State Park

Location: From Hydeville on US 4, north 4 miles on West Shore Rd.

Lake Bomoseen, about seven miles long, covers 2,360 acres. Roads encircle much of the lake shore, with much lakeside development. The park is between an arm of the lake and 191-acre Glen Lake. A separate block to the north, sometimes called Halfmoon Pond State Park, surrounds three-acre Halfmoon Pond, with campground and trails.

Plants: The terrain is level to rolling land that was once cleared for pasture and crops. Now it's a mixture of forest, reverting fields, and marsh. The forest is mostly hardwoods: beech, sugar maple, birches; red oak and hickory in the drier sites. Also there is hemlock and white pine. Many wildflowers appear in spring and summer, notably hepatica, bloodroot, wild rose, violets, jack-in-the-pulpit, goldenrod, and asters. Woodland plants include goldthread, partridgeberry, wintergreen, royal fern, and mosses. Yellow water-lilies grow in pond shallows and bulrushes and cattails in marshes.

Birds: Black ducks, mallards, blue-winged teals, yellow-bellied sapsuckers, wild turkeys, eastern kingbirds, red-winged blackbirds, wood and hermit thrushes, veerys, juncos, towhees.

Camping: 65 sites at Bomoseen, 69 at Halfmoon; each includes 10 lean-tos.

Hiking: About 10 miles of trails, including nature trails.

Fishing: Brook and brown trout, yellow perch, northern pike, chain pickerel, largemouth and smallmouth bass, bullhead.

For further information contact: Bomoseen State Park, RFD 1, Box 2620, Fair Haven, VT 05743. ☎ (802) 265-4242.

Branbury State Park

Location: From Middlebury, south 7 miles on US 7, 2 miles south on SR 53.

This small park on 985-acre Lake Dunmore is a convenient base for hiking in the Green Mountain National Forest. It's close to the Long Trail and several high peaks. It has a nature trail and a park naturalist in the summer. There is also a scenic, rather steep, hiking trail to a viewpoint in the National Forest.

Camping: 43 sites, including three lean-tos.

Fishing: Rainbow trout, landlocked salmon, lake trout, smelt, yellow perch, northern pike, largemouth and smallmouth bass, and bullhead.

For further information contact: Branbury State Park, RFD 2, Brandon, VT 05733. ☎ (802) 247-5925.

Burton Island State Park

Location: From St. Albans Bay, 3½ miles southwest on local roads to Kamp Kill Kare State Park.

This island in Lake Champlain has a 100-slip marina with power hookups and other facilities, making it a popular stop for cruisers. The island was once used for dairy and sheep farming. Now the fields are reverting and forest has reappeared on the higher ground.

The island has an abundant bird population, as well as deer and small mammals. A nature trail explains the island's history and describes its present flora and fauna. A naturalist is in residence mid-June through Labor Day and offers walks and talks.

Camping: 42 sites, including 22 lean-tos.

For further information contact: Burton Island State Park, Box 123 St. Albans Bay, VT 05481. ☎ (802) 524-6353.

Button Bay State Park

Location: From Vergennes, ½ miles south on SR 22A,
6½ miles northwest on local roads.

Button Bay is on Lake Champlain. No doubt most visitors come for water-based recreation, but the site is noteworthy for its geological features – fossils of coral and sea plants from the period when this area was covered by a tropical sea. It is also a convenient base for visits to the Lower Otter Creek and Dead Creek Wildlife Management Areas.

The site is largely wooded with mixed hardwoods and conifers, including mature hemlock, maple, and beech.

Camping: 72 sites, including nine lean-tos.
Boating: Ramp. Rentals.

For further information contact: Button Bay State Park, RFD 3, Box 570, Vergennes, VT 05491. ☎ (802) 475-2377.

Calvin Coolidge State Forest

From SR 100 at Plymouth, Southwest of Rutland, north 2 miles on SR 100A.

The Forest is made up of several blocks, irregular in shape, their largest boundary-to-boundary dimensions less than two miles. In general, all the blocks are forested with a mix of red spruce, hemlock, balsam fir, yellow and white birches, beech, and sugar maple, with some Norway spruce and pine plantations.

Special Features

Shrewsbury Peak, 3,720 ft., northwest of Plymouth is one of the highest points in the forest. A trail leads to the summit with connecting trails meeting the Appalachian and Long trails.

Tinker Brook Natural Area, 45 acres, is about two miles southwest of Shrewsbury Peak, reached by SR 100 and local roads. Its pristine habitat features an old-growth stand of large red spruce and hemlock and the Tinker Brook ravine.

Killington Peak, 4,235 ft., is the highest in the forest and second only to Mt Mansfield in Vermont. Driving northwest on US 9 from Rutland, pass through Mendon, turn right on Wheelerville Rd. and continue four miles to the trailhead. The round trip is about seven miles. The gondola and ski lift operates after the snow leaves, for those who don't wish to hike. The view from the top is superb, despite the towers, gondola terminal, and restaurant. The Appalachian and Long trails cross the mountain.

Camping: At the recreation area, 60 sites including 35 lean-tos.
Hiking/Backpacking: Trailside camping is permitted in some areas. Principal trails are the combined Appalachian and Long trails, the Shrewsbury and Killington peaks trails, and numerous side trails. Trails connect with other state lands.
Hunting: Deer, bear, snowshoe hare rabbit, turkey, and grouse.
Ski touring/Skiing/Snowmobiling: Skiing on Killington. Ski touring, snowmobiling on trails and unplowed roads. Map available.

For further information contact: Calvin Coolidge State Forest, HCR Box 105, Plymouth, VT 05056. ☎ (802) 672-3612.

Camel's Hump Forest Reserve

Location: From the McCullough Highway, SR 17, about 6 miles west of Iras-ville, north to the Winooski River. South access on SR 17.

*W*ithout a doubt this is a hiker's paradise. the Long Trail crosses the forest north to south. SR 17 W from Irasville is access to several nordic and cross-country ski areas. It climbs to Appalachian Gap, elevation 2,365 ft., just north of the Green Mountain National Forest (see entry). At the top is a parking area and an overlook; the view is attractive but not sweeping. The Long Trail crosses here, going north; the first bit is a rock scramble.

Plants: Steep terrain didn't dissuade the loggers who clear-cut many of the slopes in the 1800s, while more acres were denuded by fire. Now protected are three natural areas: a pristine stand of northern hardwoods on the west slope; a boreal forest of old-growth balsam fir; and the alpine tundra at the summit. Several thousand acres are now pine and spruce plantations, while others are in stages of natural succession with birch, beech, and maple creating color in the fall.

Wildlife: The Reserve has comparable fauna to that found in the Green Mountain National Forest. Birds include species favoring wetlands and forest more than those that soar along the ridges. Mammals include black bear, porcupine, beaver, raccoon, red fox bobcat, gray squirrel, chipmunk mink, otter, and an occasional coyote. Deer are present but not in great numbers because of the heavy tree cover.

Hiking/Backpacking: The trails up Camel's Hump are among the most popular in Vermont for day hikes. Each of the two principal trails offers about a seven mile round trip, with a vertical rise of over 2,600 ft. The Long Trail is favored by backpackers. Shelters are spaced along the Route from SR 17 to the north boundary. Trailside camping is permitted except in the Research Area adjacent to Burrows Trail and in the Gleason Brook Drainage Area.

Hunting: Bear, deer, small game.

Fishing: Some brook trout fishing in mountain streams, but most of the action is in the Winooski and other valley rivers.

Canoeing: The Winooski River can be canoed for most of its length from Montpelier to Lake Champlain, with a few dams that require portages. Where the river cuts through the Green Mountains be-tween rock cliffs, the current is strong, and there is one ¾-mile portage.

Ski touring: Ski trail in the northwest sector.

For further information contact: Department of Forests, Parks, & Recreation, 103 South Main St., 10 S., Waterbury, VT 05676. ☎ (802) 828-3375.

Cornwall Swamp Wildlife Management Area

Location: From US 7 about 7 miles south of Middlebury, east through West Salisbury and Salisbury to covered bridge.

The covered bridge, built in 1865, has a 136-ft. span. A sign posted inside invites you to join the society dedicated to preservation of such bridges. Otter Creek here is about 35 ft. wide and deep enough for canoeing, although a mat of litter has accumulated at the bridge.

Most of the Wildlife Management Area is just north of here, including wetlands on the west side of the creek. There are five miles of trails, and a posted sign asks that visitors stay on the trails.

Hunting: Deer, grouse, woodcock, waterfowl.

For more information contact: Cornwall Swamp, c/o Dept. of Fish and Wildlife, Waterbury Complex, 10 S. Waterbury, VT, 05676. ☎ (802) 828-3375.

Elmore State Park

Location: 20 miles north on SR 12.

The Park has frontage on the north end of 224-acre Lake Elmore. Most of the shoreline is privately owned, with increasing development. Most visitors come for camping and water-based recreation. Much of the surrounding area is hilly to mountainous forest, privately owned but available for hiking and ski touring. Base elevation at the Park is about 1,000 ft. A 1½ mile trail ascends 2,608-ft. Mount Elmore.

Camping: 60 sites, including 13 lean-tos.
Boating: Ramp. Rentals.

For further information contact: Elmore State Park, Box 93, Lake Elmore, VT 05657. ☎ (802) 888-2982.

Emerald Lake State Park

Location:From Manchester, Rutland, 22 miles N on US 7.

*E*levation at the valley is about 1,000 ft. The nearby Dorset Area Trails lead to 3,770-ft. Dorset Peak and 3,230-ft. Mt. Aeolus. There is also a nature trail that explains, among other things, why the older rock of the Taconic Mountains is on top of younger rock.

Camping: 105 sites, including 36 lean-tos.

For further information contact: Emerald Lake State Park, PO Box 485, East Dorset, VT 05253. ☎ (802) 362-1655.

Gifford Woods State Park

Location: The junction of US 4 and SR 100.

*T*he Park itself isn't much more than an attractive wooded camp-site, but it's a good base for other exploring. Close by is Sherburne Pass, where the Long Trail and Appalachian Trail part company. Also nearby are the Pico and Killington ski areas and trout and bass fishing in Kent Pond.

Camping: 47 sites, including 21 lean-tos. Season is Memorial Day weekend through Columbus Day weekend. Reservations available.

For further information contact: Gifford Woods State Park, Killington, VT 05751. ☎ (802) 775-5354.

Green Mountain National Forest

Location: From the VT/MA border to about half the length of Vermont.

*T*he Green Mountains are said to be Vermont's spine, stretching north to south. The Long Trail following the ridge is America's oldest long-distance hiking route. It was conceived by the Green Mountain Club in 1930, built by its members, and completed, from

Massachussets to Canada in 1930. The Club still maintains the trail, many side trails, and numerous shelters.

The Green Mountain National Forest was established in 1932, 20 years after the Vermont sections of the Long Trail came into use. It began with an acquisition of 1,842 acres. The authorized boundaries have since been expanded. Tracts have been acquired when land owners were willing to sell and when purchase money was available. One of the most recent acquisitions was 12,000 acres of wooded wildlife habitat in Windham County, purchased by The Nature Conservancy and transferred to the Forest. Although other such choice tracts may be added, no large increase in Forest acreage is contemplated.

Mt. Ellen, at the upper end of the north half is the Forest's highest point at 4,083 ft. (Vermont's highest is 4,393-ft. Mt. Mansfield.). The Green Mountains are steep and rugged enough to challenge any hiker, with views from high points well worth the ascent. Terrain is rugged and diverse, with lakes, ponds, streams, waterfalls, cliffs and rocky peaks, all in deep green forest.

Wildlife

Plants: Hardwoods predominate – maples, birches, beech and oaks – with hemlock and white pine interspersed at lower elevations, spruce and fir on higher slopes. Much of the understory is dense with witch hazel, hophornbeam, striped and mountain maples, shadbush, hobblebush, blueberry, and viburnum. Common wildflowers include Canada mayflower, red and painted trilliums, sessile bellwort asters, goldenrods, bunchberry, clintonia, Indian cucumber-root, foamflower, goldthread, orange and yellow hawkweeds, jewelweed, and jack-in-the-pulpit.

Birds: Woodcock, black-billed cuckoo, ruby-throated hummingbird, wild turkey, ruffed grouse, great blue heron. Whip-poor-will, great crested flycatcher, eastern kingbird, eastern wood-pewee, American crow, black-capped chickadee, American robin, white-breasted and red-breasted nuthatches, brown creeper; wood, hermit, and Swainson's thrushes. Veery, red-eyed and solitary vireos. Warblers: black-and-white, black-throated blue, yellow-rumped, Nashville, magnolia, black-throated green, blackburnian, ovenbird, mourning, yellow-throated, chestnut-sided, American redstart, Canada. Scarlet tanager, rose-breasted grosbeak, rufous-sided towhee, slate-colored junco, and white-throated sparrow. Hawks: sharp-shinned, Cooper's, red-tailed red-shouldered,

broad-winged, peregrine falcon. Owls: great horned, barred, long-eared, saw-whet. Woodpeckers: pileated hairy, downy, yellow-bellied sapsucker, common flicker.
Mammals: Includes deer, moose, black bear, raccoon, porcupine, red and gray squirrels, red and gray foxes, skunk, beaver, otter. Bobcat, fisher, and coyote are present but seldom seen.

The National Forest has no visitor center or nature center. Wildlife biologists and other specialists are available at the Rutland Headquarters to answer questions. Nature centers are nearby at Branbury and Emerald Lake State Parks (see entries) and at Merck State Forest.

Facilities and Activities

Camping: Five campgrounds; 94 sites. About four times as many sites are available in nearby State Parks, three on the west side of the Forest, three on the east side.
Hiking/Backpacking: Of the Long Trail's 265 miles, 130 are within the Forest. Trailside camping is permitted in almost any suitable place, and there are also shelters maintained by the Green Mountain Club, located at intervals.
Hunting: Deer, bear, rabbit, snowshoe hare, grouse, wild turkey, woodcock.
Fishing: 440 miles of streams and 2,800 acres of ponds offer some good fishing for native brook, brown, and rainbow trout. Angler access is good where Forest lands abut waterways.
Canoeing: Limited opportunities on ponds and streams; some whitewater in spring runoff.
Skiing/Ski touring: Seven ski touring centers are within the Forest boundaries. Downhill ski areas are nearby.
Snowmobiling: Permitted on designated, marked trails. One trail in Woodford has been designated for ATVs (all-terrain vehicles); winter only.

For further information contact: The Green Mountain National Forest, 151 West St., Rutland, VT 05701. ☎ (802) 773-0300.

Groton State Forest

Location: From I-91, Exit 17, north 9 miles on US 302, then north on SR 232.

This is Vermont's largest state recreation area. The terrain is rolling to steep. Signal Mountain's elevation is 3,398 ft,. with several other mountains over 2,500 ft. There are many glacial boulders, ledges, and rock outcrops. The area is almost entirely forested.

About half of the visitors come from nearby, to swim and fish in summer, hunt in the fall, snowmobile and ski tour in winter. Hiking is popular. Trailside camping is permitted, but few hikers camp.

Wildlife

Plants: What is seen from the road is young mixed hardwood forest – maple, beech, birch – with an understory of shrubs and saplings and a carpet of herbaceous plants, ferns, mosses, lichens, and grasses. The forest on higher ground is mostly spruce/fir with considerably less understory.

Birds: Over 100 species have been reported. Nesting species include red-tailed and broad winged hawks, barred owl, grouse, woodcock, five woodpecker species, kingfisher, ruby-throated hummingbirds, five flycatchers, wood and hermit thrushes, veery, many wood warblers, northern oriole, rose-breasted grosbeak, scarlet tanager, various finches and sparrows. Loons visit occasionally.

Mammals: Reported species include deer, red fox, porcupine, black bear, red squirrel, flying squirrel, chipmunk, beaver. A few moose frequent the Forest.

Facilities and Activities

Camping: Four campgrounds. 223 sites, including 54 lean-tos.
Hiking/Backpacking: 40 miles of developed trails lead to various mountains, ponds, and bogs. An abandoned railroad bed has been converted to a trail; one section is open to vehicle use. Trailside camping is permitted except in certain prohibited areas.
Hunting: Regulated by the Department of Fish and Wildlife. No hunting near developed areas.
Fishing: Trout in streams; warmwater species in lakes and ponds.
Swimming: Lake Groton and Ricker Pond.
Boating: Lake Groton and Ricker Pond. Ramps, rentals.

Canoeing: Access also at Kettle, Levi, and Osmore ponds.
Ski touring/Snowmobiling: 12 miles of marked roads and trails.

For further information contact: Groton State Park, Marshfield, VT 05658. ☎ (802) 589-3820.

Little Otter Creek Wildlife Management Area

Location: From US 7 at Ferrisburg, west about 1 mile.

The creek is broad, attractive, fringed by marsh and trees, with many water lilies. From the road, which hosts little traffic, one can overlook open water and marsh. Upstream is a quiet wetland area with good birding.

Fishing: Northern pike and largemouth bass.
Boating/Canoeing: A good launching ramp at the parking area.

For further information contact: District Wildlife Biologist, 111 West St., Essex, VT 05452. ☎ (802) 878-1564.

Little River State Park

Location: From Waterbury, 1½ miles west on US 2.

The developed area of the park is near the dam of Waterbury Reservoir, an impoundment about six miles long, between steep-sided forested hills. It is part of the Mount Mansfield State Forest .

This park is a little on the unusual side – but a treasure nevertheless. Many of the campsites are across a cove from the busier day-use beach and ramp. The sites are well spaced on the forested hillside.

Camping: 101 sites, including 20 lean-tos.
Hiking/Backpacking: Several trails from the campground offer opportunities for day or overnight hikes. Trails extend through the Mt. Mansfield State Forest, to the Long Trail, and to Camel's Hump Forest Reserve.
Hunting: In the State Forest only!
Boating/Canoeing: Ramp. Rentals.

For further information contact: Little River State Park, RFD 1, Waterbury, VT 05676. ☎ (802) 244-7103.

Maidstone State Park

Location: From Bloomfield, 5 miles south on SR 102, watch for signs.

Maidstone Lake covers 796 acres and is approximately two miles long. Both shores have roads and seasonal residences. The Park at the south end isn't large, but the country for miles around is wild, largely roadless, with clear streams, beaver flowages, ponds, small wetlands, and scattered hills up to about 2,100 ft. elevation. Away from the lake, there's ample solitude.

The forest has mixed northern hardwoods. Bird life includes warblers, finches, woodpeckers, and loon. Mammals include deer, black bear, raccoon, moose, bobcat, snowshoe hare, porcupine, and fisher.

There's a nature trail. A park naturalist offers programs in summer.

Camping: 83 sites including 37 lean-tos.
Fishing: Rainbow and lake trout, yellow perch.
Boating: Ramp. Rentals.

For further information contact: Maidstone State Park, RD 1, Box 185, Guildhall, VT 05905. ☎ (802) 676-3930.

Missisquoi National Wildlife Refuge

Location: Near Canadian border of VT on the eastern shore of Lake Champlain.

The Refuge occupies part of the delta of the Missisquoi River, on both sides of the channel. The delta is low-lying, marshy, cut by numerous winding creeks, with open water and wooded swamp. Narrow strips of cropland are on ridges. The refuge was established to maintain and enhance feeding and resting areas for migrating waterfowl.

From Headquarters, a one-and-a-half-mile nature trail makes a loop beside two of the creeks. The trail is often flooded in spring and early summer. The first half of the trail is just a pleasant walk in the woods. After that it's close to the creeks, but thickets usually block the view. Inquire at Headquarters what other parts of the Refuge can be visited on foot. Some areas marked "closed" mean only to vehicles.

Canoes allow for a relaxing sightseeing trip, but bring your own. There is no place to rent them.

The Refuge doesn't have a great number of visitors. The majority of the visitors come during summer, but waterfowl numbers are low at this time. It's a pleasant stop, but don't make a long detour.

Wildlife

Birds: A checklist of 34 species is available. The largest concentrations of waterfowl occur in April, September, and October. The most numerous nesting species are black duck, mallard, wood duck, and common goldeneye, with a few blue-winged teal and hooded merganser. Other nesting species include great blue heron, American bittern, common moorhen, and many songbirds. Seasonally abundant or common waterfowl and shorebirds include pied-billed grebe, green heron, black-crowned night-heron, Canada goose, green-winged teal, northern pintail, northern shoveler, gadwall, American pigeon, canvasback, ring-necked duck, lesser scaup, common merganser, Virginia rail, American coot, killdeer, greater yellowlegs, spotted sandpiper.
Mammals: Checklist of 34 species available. Deer are common, as are otter, red fox, meadow vole, white-footed mouse, beaver, red and gray squirrels, and cottontail. During high water in April and May, deer may be forced onto higher ground, with as many as 30 in a group.

Activities

Hunting: Special regulations. Waterfowl, deer, upland game.
Fishing: River and lake. Walleye, catfish, bullhead, muskellunge, pumpkin-seed, crappie, salmon, northern pike, carp, smallmouth and largemouth bass, yellow perch.
Boating/Canoeing: Ramp on SR 78, two miles below junction with Dead Creek. The Missisquoi is navigable by canoes for almost 70 miles, from North Troy to Lake Champlain, an upper section passing through Canada. Some rapids, dams, and unrunnable drops.

For further information contact: National Wildlife Refuge, PO Box 163, Swanton, VT 05488. ☎ (802) 868-4781.

Mt. Mansfield State Forest

Location: From Stowe on SR 100, NW on SR 108.

This is part of Vermont' s famous ski country. The popular mountain has been nastily scarred by the clear-cut slopes, more conspicuous in summer than winter. People look up from the valley to see the profile of a reclining giant's face, its features labeled on maps: Adam's Apple, The Chin, The Nose, The Forehead. In the warm months, many hike or drive to the top for the splendid views. Some features can be seen only by walking: Smugglers Cave, Lake of the Clouds, Bear Pond, and Cave of the Winds.

Hikers and backpackers will delight in this incredible hiking country. More than 40,000 visitors per year walk around the Mt. Mansfield summit, a considerable threat to its delicate plant life. No such crowds are on the Long Trail as it follows the peaks southward through the northern sector of the Forest. It then veers to the west, passing the Bolton Valley Ski Area. Side trails link it to the trail complex in the Little River sector. Portions of the trail are steep, rough, and difficult.

Wildlife

Birds: Species noted at lower elevations include yellow-bellied sapsucker, veery, Swainson's and hermit thrushes, solitary vireo, black-throated blue and black-throated green warblers, red breasted nuthatch, brown creeper, winter wren, golden-crowned kinglet, scarlet tanager, ruffed grouse, American woodcock. Near timberline: gray-cheeked thrush, blackpoll warbler, slate-colored junco, white-throated sparrow, and common raven. Hawks are aloft in migration season.
Mammals: Snowshoe hare, porcupine, gray fox, squirrel, cottontail, black bear, bobcat, and deer.

Activities

Camping: *Smuggler's Notch State Park*, on the road from Stowe, has 38 sites, 14 lean-tos. *Underhill State Park*, reached from Essex Junction (9 miles east on SR 15, 8 miles east on local roads too steep for trailers, including 4 miles of gravel) has 14 sites, 11 lean-tos. Little River State Park has 101 sites, 20 lean-tos.

Hiking/Backpacking: One of the most attractive segments of the Long Trail. Many trails for day hikes. Trailside camping is permitted except in the Smugglers Notch Ski Area and Moscow Tree Seed Orchard.

Boating: Reservoir.

Ski touring: Many trails throughout the area.

Skiing: Mt. Mansfield Ski Area in Stowe.

For additional information contact: Mt. Mansfield State Forest, RFD 1, Stowe, VT 05672. ☎ (802) 253-4014.

Pine Mountain Wildlife Management Area

Location: South of US 302, about 4 miles east of West Groton.

Pine Mountain, 1,492 ft., is at the wildlife management area's center. The highest point is 1,632 ft. Burnham Mountain near the south boundary. Lowest elevation is 900 ft. on Keenan Brook. Terrain is moderately rolling with some steep slopes, several streams flowing to the Wells River, and a portion of Scotts Brook Swamp in the southwest.

Wells River is a scenic stream with numerous ledges, falls, cascades, and pools. For some miles it flows close to US 302. A few short stretches are canoeable if you don't mind frequent portages.

Wildlife: Includes deer, bear, bobcat, fisher, snowshoe hare, grouse, wood duck, woodcock, occasional moose, and one active beaver colony.

For further information contact: District Wildlife Biologist, 254 N. Main St., Barre, VT 05641. ☎ (802) 828-2454.

Plymsbury Wildlife Management Area

Location: About 1 mile northeast of North Shrewsbury.

This area adjoins a block of Calvin Coolidge State Forest on the northern end. The area is between the two portions of the Green Mountain and Finger Lakes National Forest, on the west slope of the mountains. Terrain is hilly, gentle to moderate slopes, with several crests near 2,400 ft. elevation. It has two principal watercourses: Great Roaring Brook crosses the southern third, Tinker Brook the northeast corner. Neither is canoeable, nor is either rated high as a fishery, although there are trout in Great Roaring Brook.

Wildlife: Includes deer, bear, fisher, red fox, coyote, bobcat, and raccoon. Beaver impoundments are along Great Roaring Brook. Moose have been seen. Small numbers of waterfowl visit the area: black duck wood duck, mallard, common and hooded mergansers.

Because of easy access, the wildlife management area and nearby Forest have tremendous recreational use, chiefly by local residents. Primitive camping, hiking, hunting, fishing, birding are possible activities. Annual snowfall is about 120 inches with snow cover lasting about 100 days. This attracts cross-country skiers and snowmobilers.

For additional information contact: District Wildlife Biologist, Pittsford Academy, RD # 1, Pittsford, VT 05763. ☎ (802) 483-2300.

Putnam State Forest

Location: From Waterbury Center on SR 100, turn right at post office sign.

The Forest has several separate blocks. The one of chief interest has the trail to Mt. Hunger, a 3,620-ft. peak in the Worcester Range. The trail extends south to White Rock Mountain and north along the crest of the range.

Trailside camping is permitted. Nearby is the Little River State Park campground in Mt. Mansfield State Forest.

For more information contact: Putnam State Forest, c/o Dept. of Forests, Parks & Recreation, Waterbury Complex, 10 S. Waterbury, VT 05676. ☎ (802) 828-3375.

Quechee Gorge State Park

Location: On US 4, 3 miles west of I-89.

The walls of the gorge, steep to almost vertical, have plants ranging from grasses to stunted trees clinging to ledges and crevices. Surrounding the gorge is a northern hardwood forest with intermixed conifers: hemlock, beech, sugar and red maple, red spruce, white and red pines, and yellow birch. In the understory are mountain maple, hobblebush, beaked willow, bush honeysuckle, and witch hazel. Seasonal wildflowers include columbine, bishop's cap, harebell, flowering raspberry, little cinquefoil, fringed loosestrife, blunt-leaved sandwort, ground ivy, purple nightshade, violets, and asters.

Camping: 30 sites, including four lean-tos.
Hiking: A one mile loop trail provides fine views of the gorge from above and below, passing through forest, crossing streams.
Fishing: Brook, rainbow, and brown trout.

For further information contact: Quechee Gorge State Park, RD, White River Jct., VT 05001. ☎ (802) 295-2990.

Townshend State Park

Location: From Brattleboro, about 17 miles north on SR 30.

The US Army Corps of Engineers has dammed the West River, backing up a long, narrow pool. The State Park is below the dam. The Corps' Recreation Area offers swimming, boating, and fishing; the Park has camping and hiking.

Camping: 34 sites.
Hiking/Backpacking: Trailside camping is permitted.
Fishing: Rainbow and brown trout.
Swimming: Beach at Corps Recreation area.
Boating: Ramp at Corps Recreation Area.

Canoeing: West River.

For further information contact: Townshend State Park, Route 1, Box 299, Newfane, VT 05345. ☎ (802) 365-7500.

Victory Basin Wildlife Management Area

Location: From St. Johnsbury, east on US 2 to North Concord, then north on local road.

The Victory Basin Wildlife Management Area is part of one of the largest wetland-wilderness areas in the Northeast Kingdom (the local name of the Northeast Highlands). The land is generally flat and wet, with occasional ridges and hills. Elevations range from 1,100 to 1,400 ft.

Birds: Nesting species include mallard, black duck, wood duck, and hooded merganser. Upland species include several rather uncommon in Vermont, such as Canada jay, olive-sided flycatcher, black-backed three-toed woodpecker, rusty blackbird, pileated woodpecker, spotted sandpiper, and the common snipe.
Mammals: Moose are found here year round. Other species noted include black bear, coyote, red fox, and an occasional bobcat.
Camsite: No campsites available.
Hiking: Unmaintained logging road and bushwhacking.
Hunting: Deer, snowshoe hare, grouse, woodcock.
Fishing: Brook trout.
Canoeing: Canoe access.

For further information contact: District Wildlife Biologist, 180 Portland St., St. Johnsbury, VT 05819. ☎ (802) 748-8787.

Wenlock Wildlife Management Area

Location: From Island Pond, just under 8 miles east on SR 105.

Elevations along the Nulhegan River are about 1,000 ft. Most of the county is hilly to mountainous, with several peaks rising above 3,000 ft. The Wenlock Wildlife Management Area occupies lowlands along the river and its tributaries, including bogs and beaver ponds, with a few knolls and ridges about 1,400 ft. elevation. Much of the site is spruce/fir forest, with a few hardwood knolls.

Moose Bog is one of Mother Nature's most incredible creations. There is a dirt access road, reached by a track to the right about 0.2 miles from the highway. After about half a mile look left for a trail to take you to Moose Bog. Sphagnum moss has formed a floating mat thick and strong enough to support shrubs – chiefly heath species such as leatherleaf, Labrador tea, bog rosemary, bog laurel, and cranberry. Pitcher plant and sundew are also seen.

Birds: Nesting and migratory waterfowl include mallard, black duck, goldeneye, ring-necked duck. Breeding species include spruce grouse, three-toed black-backed woodpecker, Canada jay, Cape May warbler. Other notable species include boreal chickadee, rusty blackbird, yellow-bellied flycatcher, Swainson's thrush, Tennessee and blackpoll warblers, Lincoln's sparrow, white-winged crossbill.
Mammals: Deer population is high, especially in winter. Moose are present most of the year. Black bear are often here. Snowshoe hare are abundant. Other species include beaver, fisher, red fox, coyote, and bobcat.
Camping: At nearby Brighton State Park 84 sites are available.
Hunting: Mainly for upland game that wanders into the area.
Fishing: Trout populations in the river and beaver ponds.
Canoeing: The river is canoeable from Nulhegan Pond to its end, but the portion just below the pond is narrow, and one Class IV section is often portaged.

For further information contact: District Wildlife Biologist, 180 Portland St., St. Johnsbury, VT 05819. ☎ (802) 748-8787.

Willoughby State Forest

*Location: On the south end of Lake Willoughby,
extending almost to US 5.*

If you plan to hike here, get a trail map first. Because of Vermont's strange sign rules, trailheads aren't easy to find. The trails are blazed.

The Forest has two parts. The smaller, on the east side of the lake, includes 2,751-ft. Mt. Pisgah. Route 5A follows the lake shore. From here the mountain's flank rises steeply to vertical rock cliffs. The Mt. Pisgah Trail begins at an inconspicuous trailhead on the highway, where there's no parking, and ends south of the lake. It's a challenging hike, rewarded with some breathtaking vistas.

The larger part of the Forest is west of the lake. Then the state acquired 5,000 acres to unify the tract, giving it control of the forest around Mt. Pisgah and its twin peak across the lake, Mt. Hor. Two other prominent peaks in this portion are Bartlett Mountain, southeast of Mt. Hor, and Wheeler Mountain at the northern tip of the site. Facing the cliffs of Mt. Pisgah are the cliffs below Mt. Hor. Arctic flora are said to grow on these cliffs.

Elsewhere the slopes are generally moderate to steep. This portion has a network of trails, including loops around a cluster of ponds: Marl, Duck, Blake, Vail, and Bean.

Plants: Generally young forest, mixed hardwoods at lower elevations, red spruce and balsam fir on upper slopes. Blueberry and blackberry are common. Many wildflowers and ferns.
Birds: Species observed include boreal chickadee, brown creeper, American goldfinch, red crossbill, great crested flycatcher, ruffed grouse, cedar wax-wing, various raptors, and warblers.
Mammals: Deer, bear, porcupine, fisher, bobcat, beaver, snowshoe hare, cottontail, red and gray squirrels, and chipmunk.
Hiking/Backpacking: Trailside camping is permitted except in the cliff area and on the west shore of the lake.
Fishing: Salmon, rainbow and lake trout, yellow perch in the lake;
Boating: State ramp on Lake Willoughby.
Ski touring/Snowmobiling: Locals will tell you that this area has some of the best snowmobiling trails in the state.

For further information contact: District Forester, Department of Forests, Parks & Recreation, 180 Portland St., St. Johnsbury, VT 05819. ☎ (802) 748-4890.

Woodford State Park

Location: From Bennington, 10 miles east on SR 9.

This park on a small reservoir is within the Green Mountain National Forest, at an elevation of 2,400 ft. The park is surrounded by a network of National Forest trails, with trailheads on SR 9 both east and west of the site. The Long Trail crosses the highway between Bennington and the Park. The Prospect Mountain Ski Area is nearby.

Facilities/Activities: Includes 103 campsites, including 16 lean-tos. Reservations available.

For further information contact: Woodford State Park, RFD Bennington, VT 05201. ☎ (802) 447-7169.